GRASSROOTS STRATEGY

Cultivating B2B Growth from the Ground Up

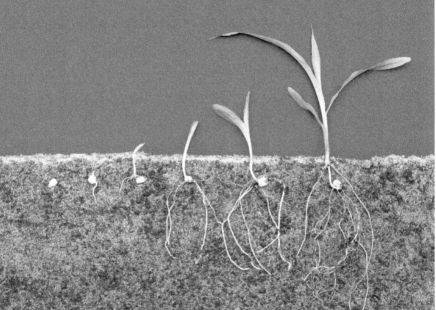

Jeff Bennett | Darrin Fleming

Table of Contents

Foreword

Grassroots strategy works! How do I know this? As Chief Strategy Officer and Chief Marketing Officer of Honeywell, I was part of the team that, along with the authors, created Grassroots Strategy over 15 years ago.

Having lived the process from the beginning, I can tell you that the impact of Grassroots Strategy on a company is nothing less than transformational. What does that mean? Several things.

Over time, you will change the **culture and fundamental capabilities** of your organization from the ground up. This critical and transformative way of thinking will become part of the fabric of your culture. Change will happen organically as more of your organization becomes more capable of truly understanding their customer's needs, and WHY they value certain product or service attributes over others.

Your **income statement** will change in ways you won't achieve by approaching strategic marketing the way most companies do. Your prices will go up because you'll learn fundamentals of pricing to value. Your costs will go down because you will target segments of customers who are willing to pay for the value you deliver. Your sales per salesperson will go up due to higher hit rates and your sales costs as a percentage of revenue will go down because they will no longer be calling on everyone.

While marketing will become more important, your **marketing costs** as a percentage of revenue may well go down because your marketing team isn't "throwing spaghetti at the wall" to see what sticks. Instead, their programs are targeted to those customers who value what you offer and are willing to pay for it. Your research and development (R&D) team will become more productive as your engineers become conversant in what customers need and value. And they will be happy that their designs are actually purchased and really valued by the customers.

Your **Cost of Goods Sold** (COGS) will go down as you stop trying to make everything for everyone and start managing your product line more strategically. This alone accomplishes many things. It will drive significant reductions in your direct materials purchases as you concentrate your buy. Your asset utilization will go up as you reduce product line complexity in your plants. And your cash flow will improve as you reduce your inventory requirements.

You will become more **innovative** and learn more deeply how to create value for your customers because of the "Flywheel Effect." You will find ways to "wrap more around your products" and transform your products into value-creating offerings, sometimes with network effect economics.

In addition, you will become much more proficient at innovating your **business models**, the recipe for how you make money. This will be made possible through a deep economic understanding of your customers, how they make money, and how you can make money serving them.

Lastly, you will be able to concentrate all of your functional spending and focus on the customer, which results in enormous **economic power.** By using customer value as the lens through which you coordinate your functional efforts, you will eliminate wasted operations and dramatically improve the efficiency of everything else.

At Honeywell, we deployed Grassroots Strategy and used these principles to rebuild our strategic and marketing teams from the ground up. We included our functional colleagues from R&D, engineering, supply chain, finance, production, sales, and senior business leadership and before long, these concepts became just the way we did business.

Working with Amphora for over a dozen years was a pleasure. Together, we traveled the world teaching and practicing these principles and in the process, creating enormous value for our shareholders. We grew profitably, attracted and developed great talent who have gone on to be highly successful, and our stock price grew dramatically.

If you want to truly differentiate your company, read, use, and deploy Grassroots Strategy. It works!

Rhonda Germany

Public Company Board Director:
Aegion, Integra LifeSciences, Univar

Retired CSO and CMO, Honeywell

GRASSROOTS STRATEGY

Cultivating B2B Growth
from the Ground Up

Jeff Bennett | Darrin Fleming

Preface

Accelerating profitable growth has been one of the long-standing challenges of business executives. Even today, with stock markets booming and M&A activity returning to record levels, organic growth is anemic for many companies. In our experience, the root cause is often a lack of strategy in the organization's thinking, planning, and marketing.

Many successful business leaders have built their careers on execution and efficiency but have relatively little experience making the strategic decisions that drive the top line. Lean, Six Sigma, and other efficiency-focused methodologies are fantastic at answering questions around how to do things better, but they are not suited to answer strategic questions around what to do and why.

Michael Porter, the father of modern business strategy, was so appalled by companies replacing their strategies with lean initiatives that he wrote an article called, "What Is Strategy." (Porter, 1996) One of our clients, describing the same experience at his employer, called it "Strategy Deficit Disorder."

Grassroots strategy is our attempt to fill this void with a user-friendly guide on how to think strategically about your markets, with a particular focus on Business to Business (B2B) markets.

Business-to-Business (B2B) is Different

We have found that most strategy and marketing books and courses focus on Business-to-Consumer (B2C) frameworks that are either not applicable or potentially harmful in a Business-to-Business (B2B) setting. The frameworks that we will present are designed specifically for B2B marketing and strategy, although they may still apply in some B2C cases. Here are several key differences between B2C and B2B environments we would like to highlight.

1. B2C companies typically have larger, more well-funded marketing departments. They spend money on market research and product testing in ways that many B2B companies can't. So, it is important to recognize that the quality of B2B marketing is not measured by the size of your marketing budget.

   The success of B2B marketing relies on understanding how your customers think and behave up and down the value chain. It is knowing why they choose (or don't choose) your offerings relative to their other options, or as we will describe in Chapter 5 (Customer Value), their next best alternative.

2. B2B buying processes are fundamentally different than consumer buying processes. While it is tempting to borrow frameworks and analogues from B2C marketing, this requires discretion, as it is often a mistake.

   For example, in B2C marketing, much is made about positioning, which reduces your value proposition to the one thing you want customers to remember about your product. This is driven by the consumer marketing limitations of a 30-second commercial in which to deliver your message, and the typical 15-second purchase decision window in which the marketer has the opportunity to influence the customer.

To state the obvious, this is not how B2B customers buy. Professional B2B purchasing managers and buying committees generally evaluate multiple product attributes across multiple suppliers in a purchase process that can span weeks, months, or even years.

3. Just as many consumer marketing frameworks do not apply to B2B situations, branding means something very different in the B2B world. And while brand recognition is certainly important in B2B marketing, what's more important is your reputation with customers, which is often largely based on their most recent experience with your company.

    If their experience is that you are, "The guys who over-promise and deliver three weeks late," then that is what your brand means to them. No amount of research, advertising or mapping your brand attributes and brand essence will fix that. In B2B, you need to focus on the reality of the value proposition you deliver. Get that right and the brand will follow.

4. In consumer marketing, the customer is obvious and the channels are well known. B2B strategy often starts with the non-trivial question, "Who is the customer?" Some B2B companies still think of their distributor or channel partner as their customer, which can be short sighted.

    The flipside is that in B2B, you usually cannot afford to ignore the channel customer. Providing value to the end customer will sometimes go unrealized if the channel is not motivated to stock your product or support your offering. In

B2B, an economic understanding of the entire end-to-end value chain is critical.

Our concepts and strategies are designed for companies navigating the world of complex non-retail channels, with sophisticated end-users and professional purchasing managers as customers.

Throughout the book, while we have plenty of B2B examples, we do use consumer examples when they help clarify a key point. This is primarily because the consumer brands and products are more well-known and typically require less background information. To keep the distinction clear, we have tried to articulate which lessons can be extrapolated to the B2B world.

Our Approach to Strategy

Amphora Consulting was founded by experienced strategy consultants and practitioners. Cutting our teeth on evaluating strategic initiatives, we intuitively developed frameworks that led us to ask specific questions about growth opportunities that were different than what was happening at many companies.

In the process, we realized that we could improve, sometimes dramatically, the selection and targeting of growth opportunities and importantly, turn good ideas into good businesses quickly and with more confidence.

What has set us apart from other consultants was our realization that there was nothing magical in the concepts we were using in our work. We do not claim to be mystical seers interpreting some strategy oracle that only we can understand. We simply get to the right answer faster because we have been through this process hundreds of times, whereas many executives have only seen it from the sidelines and often for only one project or company.

And that became our mission: to teach capable people at all levels of an organization how to apply strategic concepts themselves.

There are significant advantages to embedding strategic thinking capabilities throughout the organization.

1. Some of the best organic growth ideas bubble up from lower levels of the organization. Unless strategy skills are dispersed, these ideas may never see the light of day. These ideas need to be encouraged, vetted, shaped, and positioned for success. And they should only be rejected because they lack a compelling business case, not because they weren't invented in the upper echelons of the company.

2. Embedding strategic thinking skills creates a more discerning audience for top-down initiatives. Corporate dictates are less likely to be interpreted literally or met with resistance. When everyone understands and follows the process, top-down directives are less likely to cause unintended consequences because key leaders will have asked the "what" and "why" questions before implementation.

3. Leveraging this process over time will groom the next generation of general managers for success. Because this process teaches the entire organization to think like general managers, the most successful can then rise to the top and not have to learn these skills *after* being promoted to senior management.

4. Building organizational strategic capabilities can be a real differentiator in the B2B world. The ability to analyze markets and ask the critical "what" and "why" questions around customer value, segmentation, and differentiation is

in short supply. Doing this well can lead to improved returns in existing businesses and those you may acquire.

5. Senior executives are often forced to spend most of their time focused on the short term. Out of necessity, they need to manage quarterly performance and the expectations of Wall Street. Having a critical mass of people thinking strategically about long-term value to the customer can be a powerful counter-balance to this hard-to-avoid tendency.

To accomplish this, we developed a seminar-based approach that teaches good strategic thinking by having the participants apply what they're learning, in real time, to actual challenges confronting their business.

Mastering the Principles

Since 2003, Amphora Consulting has conducted Grassroots Strategy seminars for major companies in multiple industries, nearly all of them in B2B markets. We teach the basic principles of Grassroots Strategy and help project teams apply these concepts to real projects from their businesses, often presenting their emerging conclusions to senior management. For more details on this approach and how our seminars work, please consult the Appendix.

To enhance the effectiveness of our seminars, we continue refining the principles, our examples, and our approach to teaching. We have conducted hundreds of three, four, and five-day sessions with over 1,000 project teams from over 100 business units in companies on five continents. And we have worked with myriad industries and encountered all sorts of different market positions and challenges.

What we've discovered is that the benefits of the Grassroots Strategy approach are universal. The underlying concepts are not fads and do not change. They will not be replaced by the latest buzzword, and the tools ALWAYS work when quality thinking is applied.

We strongly believe that the application of these concepts cannot be boiled down to a set of fill-in-the-blank templates. We make sure teams push for real insight and do not accept conventional wisdom. The goal is not just a strategy that sounds good. The goal is a strategy that works well and can actually be implemented to succeed in the real world.

Most importantly, we have come to believe that the ability to both ask the right questions and hold the answers to the right standard is something that can be learned. Mastering these skills is like the old joke about a New Yorker's response to the tourist who asks, "How do you get to Carnegie Hall?" The answer? Practice, practice, practice.

Grassroots Strategy

The title of this book speaks to our perspective on strategy. The best strategies are not dictated from an ivory tower. Rather, they are firmly rooted in the reality of the market and leverage the cross-functional experience and intelligence of the entire organization. And once they take root, these strategic principles not only lead to better targeted growth initiatives, they provide the healthy foundation that is needed for a growth culture to thrive.

Throughout this book we take readers from strategy apprentice to journeyman strategic thinker. We will show you how to apply proven strategy tools and concepts within a framework that enables their correct use. With diligence and discipline, this toolkit will separate the best growth ideas from the also-rans. And it will enable you to redirect resources and accelerate the best ideas so they can be implemented with more confidence and deliver results more quickly.

How do we know this works? Well, our clients give us credit for hundreds of millions of dollars of incremental operating profit, and that's good enough for us.

The number of companies that would benefit from our approach is far larger than those we can reach with our consulting practice. Although there is no substitute for the full, week-long Grassroots Strategy seminar experience, we know that not everyone will be able to participate in a session. We therefore created this book as a guide for those who want to learn or encourage strategic thinking within their organization from the ground up.

This book is not just for smaller companies who cannot invest in the seminar. It also benefits managers at larger companies who see the value of improving strategic thinking, but cannot convince their leaders to make the required investment.

And we certainly hope it can serve as a refresher for those who have experienced the full program.

Whatever your situation, this book is a convenient way to share these concepts with all teams and individuals seeking strategic growth. We hope you enjoy the journey.

1

What is Strategy?

S trategy. Perhaps no other word is more widely used (and misunderstood) in today's business world. According to Harvard Business Review, "strategy" and "leadership" are two of the most frequently searched terms on their website.

But what is strategy? Why do you need it? How do you tell a good strategy from a bad one? When is it time to update your strategy? Not only does this book answer these questions, it presents a proven, practical approach for developing and testing market strategies and growth ideas.

We use the phrase "market-back strategy" to describe strategies that are grounded in the realities of the marketplace and the economics behind your customers' decisions. As one of our early clients liked to say, "Good ideas can come from anywhere. Good strategies are ALWAYS market-back."

And, since good ideas can come from anywhere, you need to enable all parts of your organization to think strategically and turn those ideas into great businesses. Thus, our process and the book, *Grassroots Strategy*.

In all but the most homogeneous businesses, trying to drive strategic growth from the top down is a surefire way to achieve mediocre performance because it will likely miss out on many of the best ideas. If all parts of the organization know how to identify and cultivate good ideas, you will exponentially improve your business' chance of achieving breakout success.

Some of our clients call this "strategic marketing" to distinguish it from the tactical side of marketing that consumes significant time and energy. All too often, B2B companies have marketing departments that are somewhere between lean and non-existent.

So, it is easy to get caught up in the tasks with deadlines and let those activities define the marketing function: printing price lists and discount schedules, updating brochures and data sheets, and planning the booth for the next trade show. All of these are important in context, but that is NOT strategy.

Our Definition of Strategy

There are probably as many definitions of strategy as there are books on strategy. So, against some good advice, let's get our favorite definitions on the table.

1. Strategy is a <u>clearly articulated</u> view of the <u>distinctive capabilities</u> that allow you to <u>win</u> in the <u>relevant markets</u>.

   And...

2. Strategy presents a <u>framework for management decision-making</u> that creates outcomes that are <u>more than the sum of marginal decisions.</u>

Compared to other strategy definitions, these are not brief. In fact, we have intentionally erred on the side of comprehensive. But these definitions contain several truths about strategy that bear highlighting.

- **Strategy must be clearly articulated.** According to a classic Harvard Business Review article titled "Can You Say What Your Strategy Is?" (Collins & Rukstad, 2008), if you can't describe your strategy in 35 words or less, why do you think anyone who works for you can?

- **Strategies must be grounded in your differentiation.** What are the strategic assets and capabilities that allow you to do some things better than anyone else?

- **Strategies must define "winning" and "relevant markets."** These are not so much answers as they are constraints on the process.

- **Strategy must actually change the decisions that people make.** Your job is not finished until you can articulate what's different under the new strategy. What do you need to do on Monday that's different and better than what you did on Friday?

- **Strategy has to be more than improving marginal decisions.** Deciding to get a little better at everything is a recipe for mediocrity. Strategy is about making choices and sticking with them, including the sometimes-difficult choice of what *not* to do.

- **Strategy must be practical and able to be implemented.** Unless you can clearly describe what has to change and what people must do differently, you are not finished with your strategy.

In brief, the two definitions combine to describe the two tests every strategy must pass to even be considered:

1. Can it be clearly articulated so that it can be communicated internally and reliably interpreted?

2. Will it actually change the decisions that people make?

The combined answers to these questions must describe what will be different once the strategy is implemented. What will you do more of? What will you stop? As someone really smart once said, "I'll know it's a strategy when you can tell me what you *won't* do."

Also, no matter how good you get at continuous improvement, it is essentially a commitment to "try harder" at the things you already know how to do. It won't help you prioritize among options and it absolutely won't get you to break-out growth. If you're focused on achieving four percent growth, no one is thinking about how to get 40%.

Too many companies find out the hard way that this tactical approach may work to hit short-term goals. But it will "work until it doesn't" and when it stops working, you will have no idea why without a good market-back perspective.

Myths about Strategy

As we have already said, the term strategy is overused and misunderstood, but it has an almost mystical quality at many companies. We can't help but think that this is by design. If "the experts" can surround strategy with some mystical aura, it will discourage potentially inconvenient questions like, "Why did you make *that* decision?"

This reminds us of a famous bit of dialog from the classic "mockumentary," *This is Spinal Tap*. In this scene, the guitarist, Nigel (played by Christopher Guest) explains to Marty (Rob Reiner), the interviewer, why one particular amplifier is his favorite (Reiner, 1984).

> **Nigel:** … but it's very, very special because, if you can see, the numbers all go to eleven. Look… *(pointing to the amp dials)*, the numbers all go to eleven. Look, right across the board, eleven, eleven, eleven and...
>
> **Marty:** Oh, I see. And most amps go up to ten?
>
> **Nigel:** Exactly.
>
> **Marty:** Does that mean it's louder? Is it any louder?
>
> **Nigel:** Well, it's one louder, isn't it? It's not ten. You see, most blokes, you know, will be playing at ten. You're on ten here, all the way up, all the way up, all the way up, you're on ten on your guitar. Where can you go from there? Where?
>
> **Marty:** I don't know.
>
> **Nigel:** Nowhere. Exactly. What we do is, if we need that extra push over the cliff, you know what we do?
>
> **Marty:** Put it up to eleven.
>
> **Nigel:** Eleven. Exactly. One louder.
>
> **Marty:** Why don't you just make ten louder and make ten be the top number and make that a little louder?
>
> **Nigel:** *(pause)* These go to eleven.

If you have questions about your company's strategy, but fear that the answer might be a bit like Nigel's, you are not alone. So before we move on to our framework, let's dispel four big myths about strategy.

Myth #1: Strategy is Top-down

At too many companies, strategy is thought to be something that is dictated from the top. Consultants with seemingly mystical powers spend long hours in a conference room near the CEO's office, and emerge with a new playbook as if divined from entrails.

Clearly, mere mortals are not qualified to play in this process, so why bother trying? Kidding aside, we know of one successful company in Virginia that went so far as to open a "strategy office" in Boston, as if the Brahmins from Beantown were the only ones capable of strategic thinking.

While it keeps lots of consultants employed, this premise is dangerous. It leaves most of the organization waiting for a strategy to be handed down to them instead of practicing strategic thinking themselves. Too often, basic questions like, "Did you consider this?" or "What about this type of customer?" are either ignored or seen as a lack of support. "Shut up and get on board" is the corporate equivalent of "It goes to eleven" and is certainly no way to build organizational momentum for a strategy.

We couldn't disagree more with the idea that the best strategies are top-down. Our experience is exactly the opposite; that the best strategies originate from somewhere else within the organization, often near the bottom of the org chart. Often, they are ideas based on an appreciation of unmet customer needs that grow out of the day-to-day interaction with customers. Good strategies can also start as "what-if" projects in the laboratory that create new product features.

This is the central thesis of our book – good strategies start from the ground up. With a well understood market-back framework, anyone in the organization can advance the strategic thinking of the company, essentially opening the spigot on untapped potential for growth.

Certainly, not all bottom-up ideas are good strategies. Many of them can be horrible: internally focused, unfeasible, or financially ruinous. Largely for that reason, we recommend a relatively disciplined process for testing ideas and turning good ideas into great strategies, as discussed in this book. But waiting for strategies to be dictated from on high is a massive underutilization of an organization's resources and knowledge.

Myth #2: Strategy is about finding a "Magic Bullet"

Oh, if only it were true! If only there were some way to predictably find the great idea that no one has thought of yet; to simply turn the crank and get the next iPod or Uber. Unfortunately, the real world doesn't work that way, and running a strategy process like it does can be disastrous.

We see this at clients who confuse merger and acquisition activity with strategy, as if acquiring a new company obviates the need to understand how you win with the existing one. We had one client go so far as to tell us his strategy was to buy companies at a multiple of six times earnings and then once his company owned them, their multiple became 10. "Why not 11?" was our first thought. But seriously, while this incredible financial engineering might work for a while, it's not a strategy. It is, in fact, a version of what economists call "bigger fool theory."

Acquisitions may be an outcome of your strategy, but they are not a substitute for a strategy. Letting investment bankers loose to find acquisition candidates without some very clear strategic direction is worse than asking a real estate agent to find you a house without thinking through your requirements or price range.

The truth is strategy requires hard work: understanding and evaluating multiple opportunities, and mining every customer interaction for unmet needs. Sometimes the simplest ideas can yield the biggest results. More importantly, the cumulative effect of consistently finding new opportunities ahead of your competition can be huge.

Myth #3: Strategy Starts with Quantified Objectives

We hate to break it to you, but determining objectives is the easy part. If you're reading this you most likely work at a for-profit company, in which case your objectives are clear: make more money. But that's not a strategy, it's the reason you exist.

Many believe the next logical step is to quantify your objectives in terms of how much more money you need to make. This may seem satisfying, but it won't get you any closer to a strategy. In fact, it will likely start a target negotiation process that may well get you farther from a strategy.

Strategy starts by honestly looking at your business and asking where you win and why. Then it requires an objective understanding of your customers and how they make trade-offs. Armed with this information, strategy begins with the search for "sweet spots," which are under-met market needs that are best met by your business.

Setting quantified objectives too early only constrains the process. You might overlook great small ideas that fall below some arbitrary revenue goal or stop before finding potentially big ideas.

Myth #4: Strategic Planning Produces Good Strategies

For better or worse, we have had the opportunity to review hundreds of so-called strategic plans over the last 30 years. The truth is that very few actually contain a strategy. The reason is simple: the goal of most strategic planning processes is a long-term financial plan. You may need this to plan the business and forecast capital requirements, etc., but it is not a strategy.

Most organizations approach strategic planning as a precursor to negotiating budgets and setting financial targets, so only known initiatives whose results are relatively easy to forecast are included. Less predictable but potentially game-changing ideas are ignored because they don't fit the process. Worse, sometimes known market forces or negative influences are ignored or not honestly addressed because "the trend line must go upward."

Our Perspective: Grassroots Strategy

Strategy, in short, is hard work. It cannot be delegated upwards to senior leaders who sit far from the day-to-day business, or to "strategy gurus" who dispense dubious wisdom with little or no knowledge of your business.

Strategy requires an insightful view of your markets and customers, and a disciplined process for turning good ideas into good businesses. Strategy cannot be reduced to templates and may not always run on a fixed timeline of your strategic planning process. Rather, it requires consistent application of a handful of principles that are grounded in economics.

The good news is that when stated simply, these principles sound like common sense. As such, once they are taught and their use encouraged, they are accessible to almost anyone.

Too many companies waste enormous resources on strategic planning without getting to a convincing, actionable strategy. Outside consultants can supplement strategies with research, analysis, and PowerPoint charts, but often fail to find real breakthroughs. The paradox is pervasive: if good strategic thinking is about common sense, why aren't good strategies more common?

Unraveling this Catch-22 isn't easy, but with a cohesive, logical approach driven by solid economic thinking, almost anyone can do it. Our goal is to demystify strategy by making it accessible to anyone with a basic knowledge of how their business works – no MBA required. Note that this is the exact opposite approach of many companies who exclude those who run the business from high level strategy discussions; including, for example, the company that opened their "ivory tower" in Boston to house their strategy experts.

Developing winning strategies for product lines or business units requires using a finite number of relatively easy-to-understand tools. The use of these tools can be taught and gets better with practice. With reasonable training, discipline, and time to think about what really matters, you can create a strategy capability within your organization that unlocks the potential of thousands of great ideas and takes business results to the next level.

Getting Practical about Strategy

The concepts we espouse work are best suited for developing strategies at the business unit, region, product line, or customer level. For companies with a single business line, this approach also works perfectly for developing a corporate strategy.

For some companies, corporate-level strategies are critical, especially if the key differentiating capabilities reside at the corporate level. Corporate strategies are also important for guiding investment decisions and portfolio management. But, for many successful multi-division companies, the corporate strategy is no more than a framework for prioritizing growth vectors and allocating resources.

In general, the more diverse the businesses within a company, the less a corporate strategy should shape individual business unit strategies. And even when a strong corporate strategy is in place, it frames the business unit strategies, but does not lessen their importance.

The Strategy Vacuum

By now you would not be surprised to read that we believe most companies operate without a real strategy most of the time. This sad truth often goes unnoticed because if markets are relatively stable, a default strategy of "do what you know how to do and try a little harder" will yield marginal improvement. We refer to this as the strategy vacuum and since nature abhors a vacuum, something other than a strategy will fill the void.

Not having a real strategy is far more common than pursuing the wrong strategy. Companies bumble along without realizing how they would benefit from developing a strategy. We are again reminded of our client who called this SDD – Strategy Deficit Disorder.

One of our favorite books on strategy is, "Good Strategy/Bad Strategy" by Richard P. Rumelt (Rumelt, 2011). Many consultants who write business books are so afraid of offending potential clients that they focus only on positive examples, leaving out the lessons (and fun) of other people's mistakes. On the other hand, Rumelt, an active 76 years old as of this writing, is in the "doesn't give a damn" phase of his career, which allows him to share some fabulous stories of really dumb things companies have done in the name of strategy.

We also like Rumelt's definition of a "bad strategy." A bad strategy is not a strategy that doesn't work, because even the best strategies are sometimes disrupted by unforeseen changes in markets or competitors. Rather, a bad strategy isn't really a strategy, but something that pretends to be one and stands in the way of real strategic thinking.

Bad strategies include:

- Fluff (slogans posing as strategies)
- A template-driven approach
- Poor strategic objectives
- Failure to face the problem
- Mistaking goals for strategies

We would add one more attribute to Rumelt's insights: focusing only on better execution. Too many companies got really good at being lean and efficient in the 1990s and 2000s, and seem to think that this is enough to compensate for a lack of strategy. Nothing could be farther from the truth.

In fact, in most industries, being lean and efficient is now a minimum expectation, as competition and aggressive sourcing have driven out all obvious inefficiencies. Six Sigma may be a great way to improve efficiency, but it is NOT a strategy.

Likewise, making a list of everything you can improve (or all the department-level initiatives you want to fund) can be informative, but it will not produce a strategy. As we've said, trying harder is usually a good idea, but frequently it is not enough. Strategy is about choosing your battles, not just fighting harder once you're in the middle of the fray. When you realize you're in a fight above your weight class, trying harder just means sticking it out and emerging more bloodied.

Rumelt defines a "kernel" as the three minimum requirements with which every "good strategy" begins. These essential elements are:

Premise	What assumptions do you have about how your market works? What are the underlying problems?
Philosophy	What are your core capabilities? Where and how do you differentiate and win?
Plan	What are the tangible, medium-term actions you can take? How do you know you are succeeding?

A strategy may contain more than these three elements but at a minimum, it must contain all three. Having more detail in one element, like a very detailed action plan, cannot make up for a lack of substance in any of the others. Said differently, strategy is the implied answers to the "why?" questions you must ask. Why these actions and not others? Why do you think this course of action will work? And the answer should be logical and fact based, and not sound like, "This one goes to eleven."

Strategy is not the plans, goals, and projections that are incorporated into individual objectives and incentive plans. Rather, strategy is the connective tissue that explains the rationale behind these goals and the consequences of not achieving them. Only when the rationale is articulated can you ensure that the plan is coherent: a systematic and coordinated set of actions aimed at an overarching goal, not just a list of things you can improve.

Strategy Starts with Differentiation

It should be clear from this discussion that strategy does not begin with quantifying objectives. Round number targets may make good rallying cries, but they are almost certainly bad strategy.

So where does the search for a winning strategy start? Differentiation. The seeming paradox is that strategies must always be tested from the market-back. However, knowing where to look starts with a clear understanding of your differentiation: the strategic assets and capabilities that set you apart.

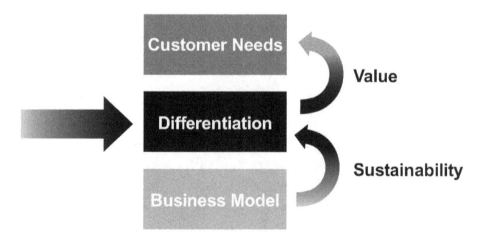

Differentiation is not the end; differentiation must create value for customers. The Grassroots Strategy process described in upcoming chapters is firmly grounded in microeconomics: how your customers define value, and how you can impact that value by solving their problems, including problems they may not even know that they have. And because not all customers value the same things, Grassroots Strategy also requires segmenting your potential customer base. Much more on all this later.

Lastly, in today's global and interconnected world, differentiation based on one product attribute may not last very long (some would argue hours or at most, days). The very best strategies are built upon business models that actively add more value over time, creating a flywheel that is very hard for competition to replicate. More on this in Chapter 9 (Business Model).

Why this Seems Hard

Beginning to think strategically is a struggle for many managers. This is not because the concepts are difficult; in fact, we believe they are eminently approachable. Rather, it is the fact that most managers have never been asked to think this way. They may have learned these concepts in school and even used them once or twice on a special project, but it's a good bet they have spent most of their career answering "how" questions.

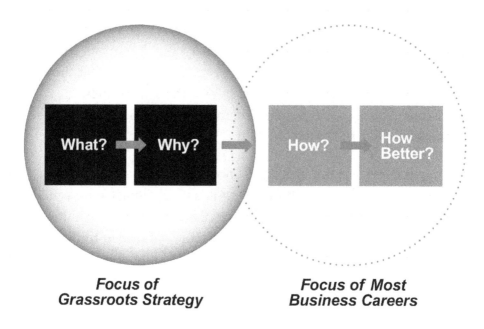

**Focus of
Grassroots Strategy**

**Focus of Most
Business Careers**

Think about it. If you are in sales, your job is to figure out HOW to sell more in your territory. If you are in operations, your job is to figure out HOW to get your plant to run more efficiently. If you are in IT, your job is to figure out HOW to get this project back on schedule.

No one has ever asked you WHY. Why this project? Why this territory? Why this plant location or product line? In fact, at many companies, asking why is discouraged. This is a sign that you are second guessing leadership and are not really "on board."

Answering "why?" questions is not inherently harder, it's just different and therefore requires a different set of tools and a different way of thinking. That's what this book is about.

The Strategic Sweet Spot

The concept is simple, and is the starting point for shifting your thinking from "how" questions to "why" questions. Your best chance of winning is at the intersection of these two realities: what the customer should want, and what you are uniquely qualified to provide.

Your natural "right to win"

SWEET SPOT

What the customer *should* want

- Under-met needs
- Customer economics
- Technical knowledge of what is possible

What you are *uniquely* qualified to provide

- Core competencies
- Credibility
- Unique assets
- IP/trade secrets

What the Customer Should Want

Note that this is not "what the customer is asking for." Getting better at reacting to customer requests may be important to near-term results, but it is not a strategy. The challenge here is to strike a balance between reacting to every customer demand and ignoring your customers because you think you know better.

One of our customers coined a great phrase for merely reacting to customer requests versus serving true market needs. He said, "That's not Marketing, that's Customering."

The only way to navigate between these two failure modes is to become a "student of your customer." This is a point we will come back to several times: you need to objectively understand their situation and their alternatives, and have a perspective on what would truly be best for them. This is critical because the ultimate test of what they "should want" is what they are willing to pay for. Knowing what you want is the easy part: sell more of what you have.

Knowing what the customer should want can be difficult, especially when it's not something the customer even knows exists. To do this successfully, you also need to become a "student of the market." You need to understand market economics, how your customers interact with their customers and how they make money, almost as well as they do.

What You Are Uniquely Qualified to Provide

This is another way to say differentiation: the strategic assets and capabilities that set you apart from the customers' other alternatives. We like to point out that this is not a core competency exercise. If you are generating multiple flip chart pages with lists of everything your company is good at, you are not holding it to a high enough standard.

Anything that a competitor can legitimately put on their list as well, needs to be crossed off of yours. A shorter, more focused, and more honest list is better than a long list that merely reflects what you say in your press briefings.

When you can find a clear intersection between these two, something that customers really should want AND what you are uniquely qualified to provide, that is a sweet spot. If you can identify those customers or situations in advance, you should be able to win the vast majority of that business. Think about the financial impact of redirecting resources, sales people, or tech support to sweet spots instead of areas where you are less likely to win.

If your first pass-through does not yield an obvious sweet spot, don't despair. This is the starting point for many established players, especially if you haven't thought about this before. As one of our clients commented late one evening, "Let's face it. There are three global competitors in our core business and we work really hard to win one-third of the time. It's no better than random."

While the best outcome is to identify an existing but overlooked sweet spot, there is another potential positive outcome. If you can identify an unmet customer need that *no one* serves well today, AND you can plausibly be the first to serve it in a way that is different than current options, you have the makings of what we sometimes call a "Type 2" sweet spot. These are generally worthy of further investigation. If you can develop an offering that is differentiating and sustainable that serves this emerging need, it can become a real sweet spot.

The Impact of Defining your Sweet Spot

Some years ago, we helped craft a strategy for a company named Automotive Finance Corporation, known universally as AFC. AFC provides wholesale financing for used car dealers throughout the United States and Canada.

Specifically, they finance many of the cars sitting on used car lots. Generally, they get paid back when the dealer sells the car, making a profit on the interest and some administrative fees. For the most part, they facilitate these transactions at used car auction centers where they can provide dealers with real-time updates on their credit lines and how much they can buy.

At the time of our interaction, both the broader automotive industry and the used car marketplace had weathered a few difficult years. In the aftermath of the financial meltdown, new US car sales dropped significantly from a peak of nearly 17 million vehicles to a low of 10.4 million in 2009 (a 39% decrease). And since cars that are traded in as part of a new car purchase are the primary source of used car inventory, their market had dropped accordingly.

Companies across the sector faced significant pressure to squeeze every drop of efficiency out of a cost structure that was spread over a significantly lower volume of transactions. But better times were ahead. By 2011, new car sales had begun to recover and better yet, as these new cars aged, they would predictably hit the used car market in two to three years. So, market conditions for the next five years or so looked positive.

Rather than just catch their breath, or worse, add back some of the cost they had worked so diligently to remove, AFC decided that the time was right to take a fresh look at their strategy. As we started our work, they had aspirational objectives around growth and some of the senior leaders had begun to think about unmet customer needs. But for the most part, they operated with a feature-based description of their offering: "We provide liquidity, transaction support, and loan processing for used car dealers." They also had a broad range of ideas on how they might grow faster than their market, but little consensus on which ideas they should pursue.

We began with a detailed look at the momentum of the business. AFC had already done much of the hard work: they had an economist on staff and had modeled how factors such as economic conditions, new car sales, and the mix of leasing and buying impacted their market. They also understood the critical market drivers. Most importantly, they documented a gradual but consistent decline in the number of independent used car dealers, their core customer base.

This work confirmed their instincts: while market conditions were largely favorable, they could not meet their aspirations just by growing with the market. They needed something else.

Searching for the Sweet Spot

Applying our strategy framework, we began to search for a sweet spot. We realized that the feature-based definition of the business made it sound like a commodity when in fact, access to capital, transaction processing, and customer support were the price of entry for their business.

The first breakthrough came when we discussed differentiation, searching broadly for strategic assets or capabilities that we could objectively claim were advantaged versus AFC's competition. We realized that while AFC was about the same size as their main competitor, only AFC had maintained its commitment to a face-to-face approach through the downturn.

As a result, AFC had more people working at more auctions than their competitor. Of the 40,000 or so independent used car dealers, someone from AFC spoke with about one-third of these dealers each month! In addition, AFC tended to hire people with significant experience in the used car business. So AFC could offer their customers meaningful, tailored insights on the industry, not just a finance package. These conversations often delivered real value to the customer far beyond the immediate transaction.

The group quickly realized the importance of these differences. Independent used car dealers tend to be hands-on owners, often working six or more days per week and almost exclusively in their own business. The good ones know their local market and customer base, but they are somewhat siloed.

They also have few, if any, resources to gain a broader perspective, and limited opportunities for learning lessons from and sharing best practices with other dealers. While not fully formed, the ability and footprint to deliver valuable insights and recommendations to these dealers was clearly a meaningful strategic advantage.

Turning to what the customer should want, another dimension of the sweet spot, the answer to the underlying question, "Who is the customer?" quickly became clear. AFC could provide a suite of services to the independent used car dealer that they would likely value. For example, AFC could help independent dealers buy the right cars at the right time at the right prices in order to maximize inventory turns and cash flow.

Franchised dealers affiliated with auto manufacturers would probably not value these services. OEM-captive finance companies typically already provide a competitive set of turnkey services, including consumer retail financing. AFC realized that they could take a page out of the OEM's playbook, bringing scale and expertise to become, in essence, the "captive for independent dealers."

Developing a Strategy

With both sides of the sweet spot coming into focus, we worked with AFC leadership to draft a strategy statement:

"We work for <u>independent used vehicle dealers</u> to improve <u>customer results</u> by providing a <u>comprehensive set of business and financial solutions</u> leveraging our <u>key capabilities</u> of branch infrastructure, dealer business model, industry scale, and breadth of corporate offerings."

Taken out of context, this could read as fluff, but each of the underlined phrases means something very specific and provides focus by defining clearly what AFC will NOT do:

- **Independent Used Vehicle Dealers.** We will not spend time chasing new car dealers, even when it is tempting to do so. We will include used car dealers as well as similar dealers in RVs and motorsports. We will not provide financing for assets other than vehicles.

- **Customer Results.** Our job is not just to make more loans and maximize fees; we strive to make more money for our dealer customers. This starts with helping them buy the right cars at the right prices so they sell faster, improving their inventory turns, and getting them back in the market for more cars sooner.

- **Comprehensive Set of Business and Financial Solutions.** We are not limited to the current set of financial products. We may choose to offer any product or service to dealers where we can provide it more efficiently or effectively than they can for themselves.

- **Key Capabilities.** We bring expertise in the used car market, scale, and a breadth of offerings that no one else brings to this market. We will continue to invest in maintaining these capabilities as the source of our strategic advantage.

With this as a guide, together with AFC's management team, we were able to prioritize the potential initiatives that the team brought to the meeting. Gone were ideas that initially sounded appealing, but were outside AFC's redefined focus and competitive sweet spot. Even more positive, we were able to identify several new, on-brand opportunities where AFC could bring a comparative advantage, such as dealer management software and extended service contracts.

Implementing the Strategy

AFC's leadership actively championed the new strategy internally, focusing on implementing both the refined focus and the new differentiating opportunities. Progress was seen almost immediately when AFC acquired Preferred Warranties Inc. (PWI), a company already supporting used car dealers. PWI offers extended service contracts and protection plans for used vehicles, and provides analytic support to help dealers price and sell used car service contracts and pool the risk.

This acquisition was perfectly consistent with AFC's refined strategy. While independent dealers would struggle to provide similar services for themselves, AFC could bring scale, expertise, and value. And while PWI only operated in 18 states at that time, AFC was well positioned to use their scale, footprint, and other resources to make PWI's services available nationwide.

The acquisition of PWI built early momentum for the strategy. Additional moves have leveraged technology and analytics to improve recommendations and help dealers track their vehicles and available credit. The financial results have been excellent: AFC's revenue grew by more than 80% over the next four years and operating profit grew even faster, up 114% over the same period!

Importantly, while the strategy work is not over, it has been greatly streamlined. The leadership team meets annually to reprioritize initiatives based on what's working and what isn't. These adjustments ensure continued alignment with changing market conditions and the overarching enterprise strategy of AFC's parent company, KAR Auction Services, Inc.

Now, nearly ten years later, AFC's strategy has survived two leadership changes, as previous leaders were promoted based on their results. The strategy remains largely intact with all its core elements still in place. That is the power of the systematic approach to building a strategy around a sweet spot.

Universal Truths about Strategy

We conclude this chapter with these universal (and sometimes uncomfortable) truths about strategy.

- **Strategy is about choice**, specifically about choices between competing alternatives where reasonable people could disagree.

  o *"Profitable Growth" is not a strategy.* Profitable growth is great and if we ask your investors, it is the reason your company exists. Demonstrating a track record of delivering against increasingly higher profit forecasts is the key to increasing your stock price, but it is not a strategy. No reasonable person would support the alternative of unprofitable shrinkage.

- **Strategy is about allocating resources**, both over time and among opportunities.

o *Improving execution this quarter is not a substitute for strategy.* Continuous improvement is generally a good idea, and it is likely necessary to keep up with your competitors. But operational excellence, no matter the form, is not a substitute for strategy.

o *Trying to do everything a little bit better is a recipe for mediocrity.* You've heard the expression, "Jack of all trades, master of none?" Just as developing a deep trade skill requires commitment and focus, so does strategy. Separating the "must dos" from the "nice to haves" is key.

- **Strategy requires an honest look** at the momentum of the business.

  o *Starting with financial projections can cover up critical assumptions.* In order to project the future, companies have to understand the past. A minimum step is separating industry trends from organizational performance. Too many companies fail to consider industry tailwinds and confuse "we made our numbers" with "we must be better than our competitors."

- **Strategy must change the decisions** that people make.

  o *Slogans and mission statements are not strategies.* It should be obvious that people don't change the decisions they make because of a plaque in the lobby or an email sent to all employees. Decisions can change when the perceived incentives and constraints are actually different. The strategist must at least begin to make this link to how the organization actually operates.

  o *The goal cannot be just better PowerPoint decks.* Even if it costs tens of thousands of dollars per page in consulting fees, PowerPoint alone does not change people's behavior. Your job is not finished until a strategy is implemented!

- Done well, **strategy is hard work.**

  o *Strategy requires different tools and different mental muscles than other processes within your organization.* In part, strategy can be a struggle because it requires different skills and frameworks than those used daily by most corporate managers.

  Further, strategy work is hard because reasonable people need a time and a place to disagree, and a mechanism to resolve disagreements that is distinct from typical corporate hierarchies and functional silos.

Summary

There is nothing magical about good strategic thinking. It is something that most people can master with the right tools, a little practice, and encouragement. By exposing your organization to these tools and teaching these skills broadly, you can dramatically improve the quality of strategic thinking and increase the likelihood of landing on the next winning strategy. That is what we mean by Grassroots Strategy.

Now that you know *what* you are looking for, we can begin discussing *where* to look.

The next chapter presents our framework for testing strategies from the market-back, and subsequent chapters step through the major pieces of the framework. The concept is to pressure test ideas against a realistic view of market needs, thereby dramatically increasing your success rate for new initiatives. In other words, sticking to your sweet spot(s).

2

Market-Back Framework

I t is our perspective that there is no monopoly on good strategic thinking. It follows that there is no monopoly on good ideas. As too many leaders find out the hard way, you cannot order someone to come up with the next great idea *and* have it by a certain date because you're meeting with the Chairman.

In reality, no one knows where the next great idea will come from. We do know that when more people think about it, the more likely it is to surface. We also know that having a structured process for thinking about strategy and potential initiatives creates an outlet for these ideas.

Too many of our clients' ideas bounce around the hallways for years with no clear process for determining whether they are worth pursuing. Often, what does get pursued is purely a function of what gets into the budget. But budgets are negotiated plans that rarely reflect explicit strategic trade-offs.

> **Good ideas can come from anywhere. Good strategies are ALWAYS market-back.**
>
> *SVP of Strategy*
> *S&P 100 Company*

Even worse is that most financial justification processes have a bias towards the known, short-term, incremental, or operational initiatives that can be readily measured and potentially produce results in the current year.

When it comes to evaluating existing offerings, the situation is often worse yet. Companies spend significant time justifying past performance and making financial projections about the future, but often lack a coherent way to analyze how a product might be re-positioned or repriced for greater success.

What's needed is a common framework for evaluating these ideas whenever and wherever they pop up. The value of Grassroots Strategy is that it engages more people across the organization and gives them a common way to evaluate improvement ideas, whether for breakthrough innovation or just fine-tuning current offerings.

Wherever they come up with the next idea, whether they're walking through a customer's warehouse or mixing chemicals in the laboratory, they can test their idea using a framework we call "market-back strategy."

The Grassroots Strategy Framework

We dedicate a chapter to each of the major steps in the Grassroots Strategy process. Let's first preview what they entail.

Before we go through the individual steps, a big note of caution. We have shown this as a linear process but in reality, it is usually anything but linear. In practice, you are constantly learning, and sometimes feedback from one step forces you to go back and re-think earlier hypotheses. This may seem frustrating, but it is clearly preferable to building a growth strategy based on flawed assumptions about how your market works.

Best-in-class companies use this thought process, formally and informally, to routinely evaluate current businesses and growth opportunities.

- **Opportunity and Market Definition.** The first step is to define your market in terms of the problem you solve for customers and implicitly, define the customer. This indicates that you need to understand your entire value chain down to the end customer, analyzing economic factors and decision-making at each step. This is also your first shot at scoping and sizing the magnitude of the market opportunity. More in Chapter 3 (Opportunity and Market Definition) on the dangers of false precision. Suffice to say that the only relevant market size question at this stage is whether it is big enough to warrant further investigation.

- **Customer Economic Value.** The second step is to understand economic value from the customers' perspective, which is not the same as the customer's value to us. In Chapter 5 (Customer Value), we discuss the importance of quantifying value and understanding the economics of the customer's business as a way to estimate their willingness to pay for features or services that you could provide.

  Chapter 5 also introduces the concept of "next best alternative" to make sure you are thinking broadly about competition. Next best alternatives include everything from direct "in-kind" competitors to alternative ways to solve the problem to living with the problem and doing nothing.

- **Market Segmentation.** Segmentation is often the most creative and sometimes the most controversial step. Here we learn the power of segmenting customers at the right level of the customer base, and the importance of segmenting based on needs. Further, we will emphasize that consumer marketing techniques which emphasize demographic and psychographic variables alone are ill-suited to B2B situations. Chapter 6 (Segmentation) includes a process for segmentation and several helpful examples.

- **Value Proposition.** This is the one place in our process where we encourage the use of a template. And although this can feel like a "fill in the blank" process, a value proposition is actually a critical test of your emerging market-back strategy. As detailed in Chapter 7 (Value Proposition), for each segment you choose to target, you must describe what's different about your offering, how the customer should value this difference, what you actually do to achieve it, and why the customer should believe you. The idea is to boil it down to a few words without shortchanging your thinking. A good value proposition anticipates the questions that a savvy customer will ask. And in B2B marketing, these answers need to be true, not just something you hope the customer will believe.

- **Business Model.** The final step is planning how to take your product to market. In Chapter 9 (Business Model) and in later chapters, we discuss the concept of a business model – essentially the delivery mechanism for your value proposition – and the importance of aligning the business model to the strategy. Said differently, how do you make money? Only after you can answer these questions should you develop a go-to-market plan that includes how to communicate to target segments, how to sell, and how to price.

In our experience, the bulk of marketing activity takes place after this last step: trade shows, marketing communications, price lists, etc. And for B2B companies with small marketing teams, it is easy to fall into the trap of confusing this activity with the thinking and strategy that should be behind a go-to-market plan.

Too often this leads to a "short circuit." Someone has an idea for a new opportunity (selling to the agricultural market) and marketing jumps straight to execution (developing a brochure aimed at farmers, figuring out which trade shows to attend, making sure the price list is current, etc.). This is done without thinking through the value proposition and business model ("What do we offer the agricultural market that is uniquely valuable" and "Can we build a business model to capture some of the value that we deliver to them"). Bypassing this critical thinking can create excess work for the already stretched marketing staff, without providing the value of strategic thinking or marketing.

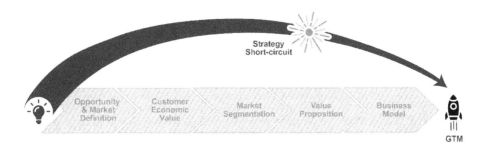

Having an organization that is confident in and comfortable working with the framework will prevent this short circuit. A market-back organization recognizes that these three critical strategy questions should not be delegated to marketing communications staff. When Grassroots Strategy is embedded in the culture, people will naturally ask these questions before spending money on marketing tactics.

1. What do you have that's unique? Said another way, what is your differentiation?

2. For whom are you creating value? In other words, who cares about your offering and is willing to pay you for it?

3. How can you make money?

If this doesn't sound like your company, it's time to throttle back the tactical marketing activities and ramp up the thinking.

Montabert Case Study

Here is a classic example from our workshops that helps illustrate the impact of getting it wrong, and then applies the framework to demonstrate what it looks like when you get it right.

Over a fifty-year period, Montabert (Montabert, n.d.) grew continuously from a small precision tool company to a major producer of large equipment used in the mining and construction industries. Profitability was driven by a skilled engineering group that developed innovative, patent-protected improvements that kept the product line among the world leaders in technology.

The single exception to this successful stream of new product introductions was a product called the Hydroville.

The Hydroville was introduced to the market as a "silent" hydraulic hammer/drill. Existing pneumatic jackhammers operated at 140 decibels (dB), a noise level close to the limits of human tolerance. The Hydroville produced only 90dB, allowing nearby conversations to take place without raised voices. Its efficient design required a 6-horsepower engine, which was much smaller than the 12 to 18 horsepower motors used on pneumatic drills.

The price of one self-contained Hydroville was set at 12,000 €. The price of a pneumatic drill was a total of 8,000 € to 1,000 € for the drill/hammer and 7,000 € for a compressor capable of powering several individual drills.

Montabert was aware that the noise levels of pneumatic drills were obnoxious to the general public and hoped the Hydroville would open a brand new market. They initially forecasted selling 300 machines per year. And the go-to-market program sent letters to every major prefect and municipal services director in France. While the machine received a fair amount of newspaper coverage, it did not generate a single sale.

Each of the firm's 27 salespeople received a demonstration unit. Customers who witnessed demonstrations were impressed but still, no sales resulted from this program.

Management felt that the high price was a deterring factor and subsequently established installment purchase and leasing plans. Again, no sales resulted.

A costly trade press campaign was launched in France but again, with little to show for the effort. After four years, Montabert had sold 223 Hydrovilles abroad and 41 in France.

Note: *Source Unknown - This version has been edited by Dr. Stew Bither, used with permission.*

Further Note: *We are sure the numbers have been disguised, but over the years, we have spoken with several people who worked for this company and confirmed that the major points of the case study are true.*

What Went Wrong?

As new product launches go, the Hydroville was a colossal failure. After four years, Montabert had not even reached its sales target for year one. Most companies would not have been so patient. We suspect they would have pulled the plug long ago on the product, the product manager, or both! But there seem to be indications that something may be worthwhile.

First, they did sell some. While the majority of sales and marketing activity was in France, they sold more than five times as many (223 units) abroad. If you were taking over as the new product manager, we hope the first thing you would do is find out who those customers were and ask them why they bought it.

Second, if you discussed the Hydroville with your engineering team, you would quickly realize that it was a huge technical breakthrough. Decibels are a logarithmic scale, so a reduction from 140 to 90 is a gigantic improvement. Surely there must be customers who would value this.

So, what went wrong? In our view, just about everything. They did not:

- Understand the problem the Hydroville solved

- Understand customer value (who and what they would pay to solve the problem)

- Identify and market to a target segment with a segment-specific value proposition

- Set a price that corresponded to value

- Make sure they had the business model to capture that value

In fact, Montabert "threw it over the fence" to the sales team without giving them a value proposition. In some organizations, you can get away with blaming the sales team for not hitting their targets, but this sure feels like a marketing failure.

Montabert's Marketing Plan

Although this wasn't good strategic marketing, Montabert did have a marketing plan. Let's look at it through the lens of one of the most venerable of marketing frameworks, the 4 Ps: Product, Price, Promotion, and Place.

Philip Kotler has been called "the father of modern marketing." He introduced the 4 Ps of marketing in his book, *Marketing Management*, in 1967 (Kotler & Keller, 1967). Incredibly, the book is still the leading textbook in MBA marketing classes and is currently in its 15th edition. So, there must be something there.

The framework is a great test for the completeness and consistency of a marketing plan but when used by rote, it can sidestep critical questions like, "Why do we think this will work?'

Let's apply the 4 Ps to Montabert and the Hydroville.

Product

It is clear that Montabert viewed the Hydroville as a replacement for an existing product: the pneumatic drill, but they did not consider the broader offering. Chapter 5 (Customer Value) discusses customer value in more detail but for now, it's essential to think beyond a physical product and consider all the services and promises wrapped around the product, explicit or implied.

Most damaging, Montabert appears to have fallen into the trap of defining its product positioning through the lens of consumer marketing. Because you only have 30 seconds to get your message across, consumer marketers are taught to focus on one unique benefit. In this case, Montabert emphasized what it wanted the customer to remember: the "silent hammer."

Not only did this cause them to overlook other important differences between the Hydroville and conventional pneumatic drills, it isn't even true. Yes, 90dB is a huge improvement over 140dB, but it is far from silent. Ninety decibels is still rock concert loud, and ongoing exposure will cause permanent hearing loss.

In contrast, 140dB is like the deck of an active aircraft carrier: conversation is impossible, and long-term damage occurs within minutes of unprotected exposure. Some sources cite 150dB as the threshold at which ear drums can rupture. Pneumatic is clearly worse, but hydraulic is still not silent.

Price

We found no description of how Montabert settled on its price of 12,000 €, but it smells like cost-plus pricing to us. It bears repeating that we believe cost-based pricing is a bad thing, always and everywhere. Prices should be based on value to the customer, not cost. Much more on this in Chapter 8 (Value Pricing).

There's another problem with Montabert's pricing when you consider the next best alternative: a pneumatic drill and a compressor. Let's say an existing job site already has a compressor that can run multiple drills and other equipment. The price to add one pneumatic drill is 1,000 € compared to 12,000 € for a Hydroville.

Although initial pricing is slightly better for a new job site with one drill, this comparison gets worse as the job gets bigger. The net result is a "reverse volume discount" where the more you buy, the bigger the price premium. How much do you think sales can do with this pricing structure?

# Drills	Pneumatic	Hydroville	Difference
1	8,000 €	12,000 €	4,000 €
2	9,000 €	24,000 €	15,000 €
3	10,000 €	36,000 €	26,000 €

This begins to explain the product's failure to gain traction. With no direction on target segments or value proposition, the sales force probably showed the product primarily to their existing customers.

Like any sales force, they probably spent most of their time with the 20% of customers that generate 80% of sales. These would likely be big construction companies. Assuming big construction companies do big jobs, they were more often than not selling in the worst possible pricing scenario where multiple jackhammers are needed on each job site that already has a compressor in place. Further, there would likely be little or no value in a quieter drill on a big job site with lots of other noisy equipment.

Promotion

Montabert sent letters to prefect directors, who are the equivalent of county-level government officials in the US. Were these administrators buying jackhammers and breaking up concrete in their spare time? Of course not. Contacting them was a regulatory-driven strategy. Montabert was hoping these government officials would mandate the use of quieter equipment on construction jobs in their regions. It's also possible that for prefect-managed projects, the government would be the customer as well as the regulator.

Strategies that require a beneficial change in regulations sometimes work but in this case, it didn't. And in general, we believe that banking on this type of strategy is risky. Most regulators aren't likely to write regulations that only one company can meet. They will either set new standards several years in advance so companies can compete to meet them, or set standards that are technically feasible today with moderate changes in practice.

In a separate example of this, one of our clients had a new fuel saving invention and was told by a regulator, "That's great. We'd love to change the regulation. Come back when your competitors can do the same thing." This is a difficult way to leverage differentiation.

Place

The fourth "P" really means "channel." We imagine Kotler's editors told him that three Ps and a C wouldn't sell and since it's still a top-seller 50 years and 15 editions later, who are we to argue?

As we mentioned earlier, Montabert leveraged its existing direct channel by giving product samples to their sales force. Thinking through the target segments for the new product first would have resulted in a better strategy to find the best channel for reaching those customers, some of whom they may not even be talking to today.

Montabert and its ill-fated Hydroville is a great example of the marketing "short circuit." They had all the elements of a marketing plan without coherent or strategic thinking behind it. Not surprisingly, the result was a colossal failure.

We'll come back to the eventual outcome as we have been able to piece it together. Spoiler alert: it doesn't end well. For now, let's review what they could have done differently if they had taken a more thoughtful approach.

An Alternate: The Grassroots Strategy Approach

Although the first step in our framework is to define an opportunity in terms of the problem it solves, remember that strategy starts with differentiation. Knowing what makes you different makes it easier to focus on the right opportunity. This is particularly true with Montabert because they already had a product. While our approach is market-back, knowing their differentiation could have helped guide Montabert toward an appropriate market.

So, what makes the Hydroville different?

- **Quieter.** While far from silent, it is significantly less noisy than a pneumatic jackhammer.

- **Self-contained.** It can operate without a compressor and without being tethered by a hose connected to that compressor.

- **Lower Power.** At less than half the horsepower, the Hydroville is more fuel efficient than a pneumatic jackhammer. Of course if it took twice as long to do the same job, it would not be more fuel efficient in total. However, this is not the case since hydraulic systems are inherently more efficient than pneumatic systems, which waste a lot of energy compressing air.

- **Lighter Weight.** We can assume this is a differentiator because the motor is significantly smaller.

- **Less Vibration.** Since noise is actually vibration transmitted through the air, this is almost certainly true as well.

- **Hydraulic vs. Pneumatic.** This could be positive or negative but since our goal is to look at this from the customer's perspective, we need to look honestly at differences in maintenance costs, training, etc.

This list gives us a lot more to work with than the "silent hammer."

Next, we want to identify which customer problems these differences might solve. Remember that this is how we define a market, although our approach is somewhat simplified in this case because we already have the product. We might call these solutions to problems benefits, but we are still a step away from determining value.

Note that as we walk through this example, we are dealing with hypotheses, so this step is not massive market research of problems in the construction industry. It's about applying common sense to what we already know and can infer. It's also not our job here to lock on to buzzwords that sound good, but rather to use enough words that our assumptions are clear and testable.

So, what problems could be solved or **benefits** be created with these differences? Here is a partial list. What else can you think of?

- Quieter might mean healthier, with less need for hearing protection among workers.

- Quieter might lead to a safer workplace, where it's easier to hear coworkers say, "Stop! You're about to step into a hole!"

- Quieter might improve public perception because there are fewer complaints from neighbors around the construction site.

- Self-contained makes it easier to transport to places with limited infrastructure. Consider that a compressor is about the size of a refrigerator and is mounted on wheels to be pulled behind a truck. If access roads are rudimentary or non-existent, you can't transport a compressor to the job site.

- Self-contained might improve access and reduce setup costs. It is easier to get in and out of small jobs and you need less equipment to transport to the job site.

- Lower power would result in less energy consumption and related cost savings.

- Lighter weight could help reduce transportation costs.

- Lighter weight and less vibration might combine to make the jackhammer easier to use resulting in less fatigue, less strength needed to operate, potentially lower training costs, and even access to a broader and cheaper labor pool.

- Less vibration might reduce the risk of unintentionally damaging the areas around the worksite.

- Hydraulic vs. pneumatic could mean lower overall maintenance costs. Although costs to maintain the hammer could be higher, eliminating the compressor and its related operating expenses will likely reduce total maintenance costs.

- On the negative side, a hydraulic hammer probably cannot be used in places where a leak would be catastrophic or extremely expensive to clean up. This is because if it leaks, it is hydraulic fluid that leaks, as opposed to air in a pneumatic system.

Remember, it is important to honestly acknowledge potential disadvantages as well as advantages. So from the customers' perspective there may be other things to consider, such as: switching costs, re-training, new spare parts to stock, etc.

Armed with this list of potential differentiators and advantages, and how they solve customer problems, we can proceed to the next step in our process: **value.**

In Chapter 5 (Customer Value), you will learn that value is defined as the economic consequences of a given benefit to the customer's business. In other words, what it is worth to the customer in currency units.

In the Montabert example, we don't have enough information to quantify value. What we can do is describe value using enough "money words" to know how we would quantify it and what data we would need to do so.

This process helps focus our efforts by giving us a good sense of which values are likely to be large, small, or negative. Let's look at some examples.

- Fewer noise complaints from neighbors may allow longer working hours. This improves the likelihood of finishing the job on time and avoiding potential financial penalties. In the extreme, this may also provide the opportunity to take jobs that cannot be done with a jackhammer today, like working near a hospital that has a quiet zone 24 hours a day.

- Less need for hearing protection might mean reduced spending on personal protective equipment. However, a typical set of headphones costs less than $100, so the savings is likely to be small. If regulations require hearing protection for other noisy equipment at the site, the savings will be zero.

- A jackhammer that is easier to use and causes less fatigue might encourage more productive time (fewer breaks to rub aching shoulders) and fewer work-related injuries (insurance, liability, and workers' compensation costs). It could also potentially expand the workforce to include those less physically endowed, thus reducing recruiting costs especially in areas where there is a shortage of skilled workers.

- Being easier to transport and easier to set up might make it feasible to take more jobs that are not accessible to a compressor. Instead of breaking up stone, tile, or concrete by hand, you can use the self-contained Hydroville instead.

- Similarly, the same might be true for small jobs where the setup and logistical costs of getting a compressor to the job site are prohibitive.

- Less risk of unintentionally damaging work site surroundings might mean lower liability and could give access to jobs where a pneumatic drill could not be used.

We could certainly keep adding to the value list, but we're guessing many of you are anxious to get to the next step: **segmentation.**

To ensure success, we must broaden the universe we are segmenting. We need to go beyond construction companies in France and focus on anyone who needs to break up rock or concrete.

Given the limited scope of this example, we will not attempt to develop an exhaustive segmentation schema as described in Chapter 6 (Segmentation). There you will learn that a segment is an identifiable group of customers (or applications) with similar needs.

For argument's sake, we have identified several potential groups of applications or customer types, the potential segments for whom the Hydroville may have value.

- **Urban Reconstruction.** These job sites are typically in populated areas where environmental noise is an issue and extended working hours could increase the profitability of jobs.

- **Remote Locations.** Remote job sites often have no infrastructure, making it prohibitively expensive to transport a compressor. Examples include building a ski station in the Alps or working on an offshore oil platform.

- **Underground.** Mining immediately comes to mind, but this can also include city sewers and subway tunnels where both ease of access and vibration are issues.

- **Rental Market.** This is a great example of a segment that does not exist today. Since the Hydroville is self-contained, easy to use, and easy to transport, it is perfect for smaller jobs. Smaller jobs are typically done by smaller contractors, many of whom rent their equipment. Since many channels that serve small contractors also cater to consumers, it might be worth testing and potentially creating a new DIY market.

- **Search and Rescue.** First responders might need a rapidly deployable solution in situations where the infrastructure is limited or has been destroyed. Lower vibration might also improve safety if potential survivors might still be trapped in the rubble, like after a major earthquake.

- **Military.** In addition to the reasons previously given, the military might disproportionately value energy savings. Since fuel is transported to the front lines by armored convoy, the actual cost per gallon consumed is a multiple of what the rest of us pay at the pump.

One of the more interesting things about segmentation is the segments we choose *not* to target. In our example, none of these potential segments applies to big construction sites. And yet, that is almost certainly where the salesforce spent the bulk of its time because it is where they sell most of their existing products. The lesson is to take a fresh look at segmentation when considering something new.

The ultimate test of segmentation is in the next step, the **value proposition**. Said differently, a segment is truly a segment if the customers in that segment want the same value proposition *and* that value proposition is different than other segments. The segments in this example (and potentially several other potential segments) pass the test.

To avoid making a long story longer, we have left out the **business model** step. Surely you can imagine that if some of these segments proved to be attractive, Montabert might need different sales people, different channels, and maybe even different pricing mechanisms (like "by the hour") in order to capture the most value.

Before we leave our thought experiment, let's tie up some loose ends. As the new Hydroville product manager, what would you do next? Since these are hypotheses, the next step is to test them. Conducting internet research is the easiest way to make sure you haven't missed something obvious, such as another next best alternative.

If the initial research looks positive, then it's time to speak with potential customers about their needs relative to the hypothesized value. Where there is interest, you can move to more detailed research to quantify the value. You could even conduct a pilot test to quantify value, since Montabert had already created a prototype. Most importantly, you should do all this *before* developing go-to-market plans!

Imagine doing this in your own business where you already have knowledge of your customers and their problems. Your hypotheses would be even better than those in this example. Of course, this means extra work if you're used to doing "activity marketing," but think about the payback. With a diligent summer intern, you can sort through opportunities and get comfortable with those that are most likely to be real. The cost will be far lower than years of trial and error (mostly error) because of a failed strategy.

Imagine we could do this research for Montabert. It is possible that some segments have structural reasons that prevent using the Hydroville: mining regulations, for example. But others could have been quite promising: military applications, remote locations, and small contractors/DIY rental. If Montabert chose to pursue these segments, each would have fundamentally different value propositions and go-to-market plans. Little would be the same, from pricing, promotion, channels, and sales targets to brochure content and trade show participation.

Sadly, we will never know how this might have worked. We know that a few years after this case took place, Montabert was bought by Joy Manufacturing. Impressed with the Hydroville technology, Joy launched the product in the US with similar tactics and sadly, but not surprisingly, similar results.

Since then Montabert has been bought and sold several times and is now owned by Komatsu. We believe that our approach would have led to a different result. Apparently Montabert's compact, powerful hydraulic technology really was a differentiator because the Montabert name and technology survives on a leading line of rock-crushers. Unfortunately, the opportunity to transform the hand-held jackhammer market has passed, as there are now multiple next best alternatives, including both hydraulic and electric jackhammers.

As you consider the power of this approach, there is one more thing that could have resulted in a significantly different outcome. Montabert could have run this entire thought exercise *before* spending a dime on engineering. Nothing we did required a prototype or even a sketch of the unit.

We prefer this approach because it prevents you from getting locked into a benefits list before you have tested it with customers and it allows you to find other problems. For example, if ease of use is the big issue, you would focus your design efforts on that instead of noise reduction.

So, there it is. Nothing magical, just the disciplined application of questions that too many companies forget to ask, specifically at the right time:

- Who is the customer?

- What problem do you solve for them?

- What is it worth to solve that customer problem better than their alternatives? (Value and differentiation) In other words, how do you improve their business outcome?

- Which specific customers need us the most? (Segmentation)

- How do you convince customers that your product solves their problem in the best, most cost-effective way? (Value Proposition)

Only when you have answered these questions does it make sense to develop a go-to-market plan. With practice, asking these questions will become second nature and you can avoid costly mistakes like those made by Montabert. Instead, you can make the most of your position in the marketplace and win more business in target segments at prices that reflect the value you create.

Summary

One more note before we move on to Chapter 3 and the first step of the framework: opportunity and market definition. Keep in mind that although we present this as a linear process, it is anything but. In reality it is almost always iterative. Everything you learn changes your perspective in ways that impact earlier steps, so you need to recycle through the entire process to realign with new learnings.

Also note that the Montabert example was simpler than you may face because the product already existed. Your challenge is to look more broadly at customer needs before developing your next offering. In our experience, having some sense of your potential differentiation helps create a convergence of possible sweet spots more efficiently than just generating a laundry list of possible customer needs.

This inherently iterative process can be frustrating but without having perfect knowledge and all the answers up front, we know of no way to avoid it. Our consolation is that it's better to find mistakes quickly and correct them during an internal thought exercise than to correct mistakes later in front of the customer or after a failed product launch.

As we work through the next several chapters, we encourage you to work in hypotheses. More on this in Chapter 10 (Hypothesis Testing).

Hypotheses enable us to use what we already know and move quickly to implications while remembering that ultimately, our assumptions need to be tested. It is the natural process of learning, updating your hypotheses, and adapting your value propositions that ensures Grassroots Strategy remains a dynamic, living process. And through continuous application, it will become second nature to you and your organization.

With that overview, we are ready to jump into the first step in the framework: opportunity and market definition.

3

Opportunity and Market Definition

A n entire chapter on defining your market? It's obvious, isn't it? Well, we obviously don't think so. In this chapter, we will emphasize that when looking for opportunities, a market should be defined as the problem you solve for a set of customers. Reports and analysis on existing product markets may help you understand what's going on today, but they are of little value in figuring out what to do about it. But first, allow us to start with a hypothetical situation that will make many of the points in this chapter.

Imagine being asked to evaluate two options for starting a new business within your company. Of course, a business case for each option is needed. What information would be expected in the business case?

Think in terms of what senior management would need to know to justify the investment in your new business. Most companies have a list of required information for a business case, but almost all will require at least the following four pieces of data:

- Size of the market
- Growth rate
- Competition
- Expected profitability

Let's take two hypothetical examples and decide together which opportunity we would rather stand behind and recommend for investment.

Evaluating Opportunities

As part of your hypothetical preparation, you buy a couple of analyst reports, gather other industry data, and create the following analyses.

Opportunity 1

This is a consumer electronics product. Your business doesn't currently have any offerings in this product category. The current market landscape for this opportunity looks like this:

Opportunity Size	600,000 units @ $250 = $150 million
Growth Rate	Approximately 12% per year
Competition	Sony, Samsung, and Ericson as well as Saehan and SanDisk have established offerings
Profitability	Millions of dollars of investment so far and all losing money

Opportunity 2

This is a consumer product. Your business doesn't currently have any offerings in this product category. The current market landscape for this opportunity looks like this:

Opportunity Size	$200 billion
Growth Rate	Approximately 8% per year
Competition	Fragmented (more than 40,000 competitors with largest less than 2% share)
Profitability	Gross margins greater than 50%

If you have a limited amount of money to invest, where would you put your money: Opportunity 1 or Opportunity 2?

From a traditional market analysis perspective, Opportunity 2 looks much more attractive. It is a large and growing market. It has fragmented competition, which usually means there could be an opportunity for consolidation. It may be easier to establish a brand. And with gross margins over 50%, the opportunity looks very appealing.

On the other hand, Opportunity 1 is relatively small from a consumer electronics perspective. While a 12% growth rate is attractive, it is not indicative of the rapid adoption phase of consumer electronics. It isn't going to get large any time soon and will likely remain a niche product. The competition includes very strong global consumer electronics players and they are all struggling to make money. No one in their right mind would choose Opportunity 1 over Opportunity 2, right?

Not so fast. Opportunity 1 is a view of the MP3 player market in 2000. Opportunity 2 is a view of the US retail jewelry market in 2012. Everyone (well, everyone over 30) remembers what happened to the MP3 market in 2001 when Apple launched the iPod. In fact, Apple has brought in more than $1 trillion in revenue from devices that have evolved from the original iPod (including the iPad and iPhone) (Miller, 2017), and the earnings from those devices are now larger than Apple's earnings from everything else combined (Blood, 2015).

As for Opportunity 2, jewelry stores have high working capital costs because of slow-moving inventory, high fixed overhead costs, and high failure rates. The growth rate of 8% was not a long-term trend, but rather a cyclical recovery from the disaster of 2009-2010. Lastly, no one has been successful in consolidating this market and the internet is continuing to erode the margins of traditional retailers.

Meeting Unmet Needs

What did Apple see in 2000 that wasn't apparent in the Opportunity 1 analysis? Essentially, they saw a set of unmet needs in the market. Although the technical problem of digital music had been solved, there were still some fundamental issues hindering mass adoption of MP3 players.

First, it was very difficult to get the music onto the MP3 devices. If consumers wanted to take the high road, they had to copy the music from a CD to a computer, provided they had the right hardware. Next, they had to convert the music files from WAV format to MP3 format, which required software and some technical savvy. Then they had to copy the music from the computer onto an MP3 device.

The more likely scenario was using a music sharing service such as Napster to acquire the music in MP3 format. Although this was far easier, it was unfortunately, illegal. Thus, the unmet need for the typical consumer was a legal, easy, and fun way to acquire portable music.

The problem wasn't the MP3 devices or the product. It was the music delivery mechanism. Apple didn't try to compete with the other MP3 manufacturers on a feature basis. As urban legend has it, an engineering teardown of the original iPod would likely have shown that the device was made almost entirely with 3-year old technology, in a consumer electronics market with a technology half-life of 12 to 18 months.

Instead, they opened up the majority of the market that wasn't available to the other MP3 manufacturers by solving the market's unmet needs: making portable music easy, legal, and fun. They didn't win with a better device, they won with a disruptive business model that leveraged their iTunes content delivery platform to solve real customer problems.

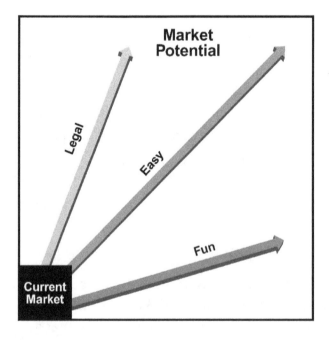

Learning from this admittedly extreme example, to properly evaluate the business case for an opportunity, you must first:

- Understand the dynamics of the market (insights, not just data!)

- Identify any unmet needs, and understand why they are not being met by current offerings

- Look for ways to create sustainable differentiation by addressing those unmet needs better than other alternatives

- Measure the potential size and profitability of the opportunity, not last year's market for existing products and customers

Don't waste time looking in the rearview mirror at today's market and competitors to determine your business strategy. At best, it will set you up to be late to market with a product that is not quite as good as the current competitors and with a higher cost structure. This is a sure recipe for failure!

Market Definition

It is impossible to define a market opportunity without first defining the market. Investopedia.com defines a market as, "A medium that allows buyers and sellers of a specific good or service to interact in order to facilitate an exchange."

If you look for information about almost any market (size, growth, competition, etc.), it will invariably be organized by the product or service being sold, supporting the premise that a market is specific to a good or service. But to understand an opportunity, should we really focus on the product perspective? Would Apple have won if they focused on a better MP3 player? Almost certainly, not.

According to Harvard marketing professor Theodore Levitt, "People don't want to buy a quarter-inch drill. They want a quarter-inch hole!" In other words, the opportunity is about holes, not drill bits.

If you limit your view of the market to a product definition, you miss out on other alternatives the customer can use to get the hole: hammer and nail, borrow a neighbor's drill, hire a contractor, laser cutter, CNC machine, dynamite (if they don't care about the precision of the hole), or make something with the hole already in it (3D printing).

By defining your market from the perspective of the product or service you are selling, you will miss large portions of the opportunity by missing potential customers (Best, 1997):

- That aren't aware a solution exists

- That don't have access to buy the solution

- That are currently unable to use the solution because they lack the infrastructure or experience

- For whom the current form of the solution lacks benefits for their situation

- For whom the current form of the solution is too expensive for their needs

We use the word solution here because it implies that a problem is being solved. Think back to the iPod story. Did Apple think they were just entering the MP3 player market? No. More likely they would have defined it as the market for portable music that is legal, easy to use, and fun.

That's not a product view of the world, it's a view of the problem being solved. When evaluating an opportunity, you should think about your market based on how a customer would describe their problem and their alternatives, which obviously will evolve over time.

Product	Problem: Alternatives
MP3 Player	Portable music: Walkman, Discman, Itunes, Spotify, Pandora...
Drill Bit	Hole: Nail, water jet, laser, 3D printed part...
Fax Machine	Transmission of printed information: email, snapchat, text, FedEx...

Expanded Market Definition

During most of Jack Welch's tenure as CEO, he often told GE leaders to make sure their business was #1 or #2 in their market, or GE should exit the business (Beattie, 2018). So, with their job on the line, smart GE business leaders began defining their market so that their business was among the top two competitors. Over time, all surviving business leaders had done so.

But what happens when your business is already one of the top players with over 40% market share? Your opportunities for growth begin to diminish.

This began to happen to GE businesses later in Welch's tenure. He recognized the need to change his original edict and towards the end of his time as CEO, he required his businesses to define their market such that they had no more than 10% market share (Beattie, 2018). Why? Because it forced them to find room for growth.

We contend that the right answer isn't merely a smaller or a larger market definition. You should always have both. The smaller market definition is your core. The larger market definition shows room for growth and where you should be looking to expand. Here is a 3D illustration of a generic market definition:

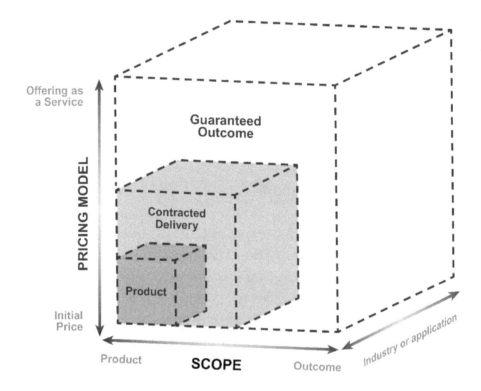

There are many ways to expand your market definition, but it helps to look for opportunities along these three dimensions, defining the market in terms of what it could be and not necessarily the smaller space in which you currently play.

1. Who could you serve?

   - Industries

   - Geographies

   - Applications

2. What could you deliver?

   - Scope of supply

   - Problems you are solving

   - Attributes of your offering

3. How could you serve them (or get paid)?

   - Payment model (initial price > price plus maintenance > offering as a service > paid for outcomes)

   - Unit of Measure for Pricing (product > solution > outcome)

The bottom line is that you need to define your market from your potential customers' perspective, based on the problem that they are trying to solve, even if you do not provide the entire solution. That allows you to identify all the alternative ways to solve the problem, find new opportunities, and identify potential competitive threats.

The goal is not to serve the entire cube, but rather to expand the space where you can look for growth. An excellent consumer example is Coca-Cola. Imagine how limited their growth prospects would have been had they stuck to a market definition of "North American cola beverages."

By adding dimensions to their cube, they have grown dramatically in diet drinks, juices, energy drinks, and sport drinks, and have explored different business models beyond the traditional local bottler network.

The Nest learning thermostat launch illustrates both the concepts of solving a customer problem and expanding the market definition or "cube." Nest Labs was founded in 2010 by two former Apple engineers, Tony Fadell and Matt Rogers (Bloomberg, 2019). They chose the thermostat as their first product not because of some broader goal of saving the planet, but for the mundane reason that the thermostat "hasn't been innovated in 20 years," to use Rogers' own words (Kessle, 2011). We might argue it had been 30 years or more since there was any meaningful innovation in thermostats.

Much has been made of Nest as a design success. And while it certainly is more visually appealing than the "wall acne" (an interior decorator term) it replaced, we believe its success is because it is first and foremost a better solution to a customer problem.

What is the problem a thermostat solves? Technically, it cycles the heating/cooling system on and off in response to a temperature signal. But what is the customer problem? Nest realized that the thermostat is a core part of a system (the x-axis of the cube) that helps a customer balance the trade-off between comfort and energy usage. Since most customers care about both comfort and energy, Nest made it far easier to balance the two.

At the time of Nest's introduction, the market for thermostats was well established. Over the 100+ years since they were first introduced, thermostats became digital, more accurate, and less expensive. But the energy crisis in the 1970s brought about the category's single biggest innovation: the programmable thermostat.

The premise was straightforward. Many people are less concerned about the temperature of the house while they are at work, or perhaps they like the house cooler while they sleep. Now they could program the thermostat at different set-points by hour to save energy when the house is empty and be comfortable when at home.

By the early 2000s, the market for programmable thermostats was well established, representing more than half of all new thermostats sold (Comstock, 2014). But here is where the customer insight came in.

Nest discovered that the majority of homeowners had permanently set their programmable thermostats on hold. According to the U.S. Energy Information Administration, only 19% of programmable thermostats were even programmed (U.S. Energy Information Administration, 2018). In other words, homeowners were receiving no more value than they would have from a standard thermostat!

Why didn't consumers regularly use the programmable feature? Because it was too difficult to use and did not fit their use case.

Most of us can relate. When you come home from work on the first hot day of the year, you just switch the thermostat from heat to cool and cold air starts to blow within seconds. Problem solved. Even though you want the system to run optimally, you probably don't want to dig out the thick instruction manual with small print, written by HVAC engineers, to figure out how to program the system.

If you are like most of us, you are thinking about dinner and want to get started on the rest of your after-work routine: changing your shirt, helping the kids with their homework, turning on the TV, and serving yourself an adult beverage or two. (No judgment; just describing our personal experience.) The last thing you want to do is mess with thermostat technology.

Programmable thermostats solved the technical problem, but failed to solve the customer problem. To solve ease of use on a day-to-day basis, the thermostat must be specified correctly, installed correctly, set up correctly, and used correctly. It only solves the customer problem when it works as part of this broader system.

This is the x-axis of the cube: thinking beyond just the product. If this isn't clear, we challenge you to buy a thermostat on your way home from work tomorrow and set it on your kitchen counter. We are pretty sure that nothing will change in your home except the charge on your credit card bill.

Nest overcame the complexity of programmable thermostats by delivering the value of programmability without needing to be programmed. The device senses when you are home and learns your patterns. It then optimizes the temperature at all times of the day.

For added flexibility, you can override the system through an intuitive app on your smartphone if, for example, you are coming home from work early. Nest also provides real-time feedback on energy usage. You don't have to wait a month to compare your year-over-year energy consumption and factor it against the average temperature to know the thermostat is working.

By finding a better way to solve the underlying customer problems, Nest successfully expanded the market. And by simultaneously focusing on ease of installation, they made thermostats a DIY item, capturing a piece of the contractor margin as well.

Until Nest came on the market, thermostats were generally only sold when a failing furnace or central air conditioning system was replaced. It was a $40 purchase as part of a mechanical equipment replacement.

Nest launched successfully at $249 (Kessle, 2011) and turned the lowly thermostat into a lifestyle purchase. It has become a foundation for other home automation devices and services under the Nest brand. Its impact on the market has accelerated since Google acquired Nest for $3.2 billion in 2014 (Winkler & Wakabayashi, 2014).

This valuation clearly reflects the importance of looking beyond current products as part of a bigger potential market cube.

Market Potential and Sizing

Sizing a potential market is easy. All you have to do is find an analyst firm that follows your target market and buy their latest market report, right? After all, most major markets are tracked by at least one analyst firm and their reports can provide the market size and growth rate with accepted precision.

But isn't that what we did earlier in this chapter when we investigated two opportunities for their investment attractiveness? Would the statistics from an analyst report have helped us make a good decision, or would they have led us down the wrong path?

Let's clarify by saying that there is nothing wrong with buying an analyst report and that analyst firms serve a very useful function. When looking at the potential size of a target market, however, an analyst report should be just one source of information. The drawbacks of relying too heavily on analyst reports starts with how an analyst firm goes about estimating the size and growth potential of a market.

For starters, they almost always define a market based upon the product or service provided. In other words, they look at the market for drill bits, not the market for holes. The work is typically performed by a junior analyst, who collects information about the market and gathers data by calling the suppliers in the market. The suppliers naturally provide information based on how they want to be perceived, and do not necessarily provide actual results unless that information is already available publicly.

The analyst combines historical data with these questionable vendor responses to project growth based on the historical growth rate. This data only takes into account customers that have actually bought the product or service. It does not include those that have knowingly or unknowingly chosen not to buy and those that have chosen to solve the problem in a different way. Market size is also based on the current pricing for the offering in the market.

Despite all these qualifying factors, the market size and growth rate are reported with great precision, so everyone feels good about the results. Here is what you end up with:

- A person that doesn't know your market as well as you do

- Collecting data from unreliable sources

- Based on a product vs. problem definition of the market

- Projecting future growth of the current market based on historical trends

- Probably ignoring a big piece of the potential market

Other than that analyst reports are perfect!

All sarcasm aside, analyst reports provide good indications of current market conditions. And they can provide an overview of the competitive landscape and current trends that are likely to continue given no other changes. Our goal is to just make sure you understand the limitations of these reports.

Innovative offerings challenge the existing market assumptions that are embedded in even the best market reports. For example, Nest likely knew that the average thermostat was priced around $40 and that the vast majority were sold in conjunction with a major mechanical equipment purchase. But was this relevant to their entry? No. They set out to revolutionize the market, triggering incremental sales and pricing to value at $249 per thermostat.

We define market potential as the sum of the value created by solving the problem at hand for each individual customer in the entire market. We will discuss how to estimate the value created for each customer in Chapter 5 (Customer Value). For now, let's consider all potential customers, including those who are currently not buying, and your best estimate of the value that they would receive by solving the problem.

Since we don't know the value created at this point, we can start with the market size in units to get a sense of whether it deserves further analysis. We might also look at what customers are paying for alternative ways to solve the underlying problem to get an initial estimate of value.

Let's walk through how Apple could have approached sizing the market for iPods before they were launched. Although estimates at the time indicated that the market was 600,000 units growing at 12% annually, Apple seemingly had enough insight to know that the market potential was far greater. While we have no idea what they actually did, there are some ways to estimate the size of a market that has not yet developed.

By value potential (preferred)		By analogy
• People who like music:	6 billion	• Peak year sales volume – Walkman:
• With computers:	20 percent 1.2 billion	16 million units
• With internet access:	33 percent 400 million	• Peak year sales volume – Discman:
• With disposable income:	90 percent 360 million	18 million units
• Ten-year penetration curve:	10 percent 36 million	
Actual peak year sales (2009): 54 million units		

One of the best ways to size an opportunity is to estimate the total number of potential customers that exist. For the iPod, that number includes anyone in the world who likes music, has a computer with internet access, and who has enough discretionary income to buy both the device and the music. That would have yielded roughly 360 million people, which is significantly more than the estimated 600,000. A 10-year penetration cycle leads to a market potential of 36 million units per year.

Another approach is to look for existing proxies. Are there other similar problems being solved, or is the problem currently being solved in a different way? Relative to the iPod, other devices providing mobile music were already on the market before MP3 players, Sony Walkman and Discman in particular. Peak year sales for those devices were 16 million and 18 million units respectively. Is an estimate of 36 million unrealistic, given the better user experience with an iPod? In reality, peak year iPod sales (2009) were 54 million units.

How precise does your sizing need to be? That depends on many factors including the size of the investment, the risk associated with the opportunity, and your starting point. Ultimately you need enough precision to ensure that you can make a robust decision about the next level of investment.

Let's say you are entering a new market. Based on available information, you estimate that the market is between $1 billion and $5 billion and you need a $1 million investment. In this case, it really doesn't make sense to spend more time and money to determine a more precise size because you will probably make the same decision whether the size is $1 billion or $5 billion.

On the other hand, suppose you estimate that the market is between $100 million and $200 million. You want to invest the same $1 million and are currently doing $50 million of business in that market. You probably need to narrow the range because you wouldn't make the same decision for a market sized at $100 million as you would for $200 million.

A simple test is to take the outside ends of your range and determine what your decision would be. If you make the same decision at both ends of the range, then you probably have enough precision. If you would make different decisions, then you probably need more analysis.

Market sizing is much easier and often more important in established markets. With new opportunities, it is more important to determine whether the size of the opportunity is big enough to make the investment weighed against the risk, and less important to know the exact size of the market.

This logic may seem obvious, but too many business people still confuse the level of detail with the degree of confidence. And old habits can be hard to break.

One of our clients was considering investing in a new business opportunity in a new market. In their presentation to an executive, the project team estimated the market to be between $5 billion and $6 billion. The executive interrupted them and asked, "Which is it? $5 billion or $6 billion?"

The team was taken aback and said they didn't know precisely, but were confident it was within that range. The executive ended the meeting by telling the team to do more research because if they didn't know the market better, their recommendation had no credibility and the company would not invest in it.

Was this the right approach? We don't think so. The executive was asking the wrong question because the decision to invest didn't depend on whether the market was $5 billion or $6 billion. The right questions would have included, "Why do we think we can win in this market?" or "What do we have that will be unique or different than others in this market," or even "Is there a segment of this market where we believe we will have a stronger value proposition?"

Unfortunately, the executive chose to waste company resources searching for answers to the wrong questions. The real tragedy is that by striving for precision, the team fell back to sizing the existing market and presented a market size of $150 million at their next meeting. Without much fanfare, the project wasn't approved because the opportunity was too small. Luckily for our client, that executive was relieved of their duty soon after this occurred.

Market Drivers

Everyone talks about market drivers, and most people can probably even name a few for their business. But why do we care about market drivers? Are they just a nice thing to include in your PowerPoint presentation during your annual business and strategy review presentation? If that's all they are, then you're missing the point of looking at market drivers.

We care about market drivers because they help us understand current and past changes in our market. More importantly, they help us understand what's driving the present and future. Market drivers provide insight into WHY decisions and trade-offs are made. This is true on both the demand and supply sides of the equation.

A market driver is an underlying force or factor that will impact market size and composition. Some examples include growth in end use markets, economic trends, regulations, technology shifts, and population.

Let's explore the difference between a market driver and a trend, as it can be dangerous to confuse the two. In essence, the trend is the result of the economic force of the driver. Trends are important, but trends almost always change and often reverse over time.

In spring of 2008, we worked with a company that used petroleum as an ingredient in many of their products. At the start of a strategy session, the CEO made the following statement to the four project teams we were working with. "Oil prices are at $140/barrel. Everyone knows that they will continue to go up. I want all of your strategic plans to reflect $200/barrel oil."

By October of that year the price of oil had dropped below $100/barrel and for the most part, has stayed below $100 ever since.

Prices even dropped below $30 at different points. Although the trend at the time of the strategy session was up and oil prices were a critical factor and a market driver for their business, using the trend alone to build their strategic plans was both reckless and dangerous.

A better request would have been to ask each business to plan what they needed to do if the price went up OR down, and to evaluate their opportunities based on different scenarios. Understand the difference between a trend and the underlying market drivers and evaluate your business accordingly.

Back to the iPod example. What do we see as potential market drivers for the iPod market? Per the earlier sizing estimate, the obvious drivers are the number of people who like music, have a computer with internet access, and have enough discretionary income to buy both music and device. It's safe to assume, therefore, that the trend and market potential were likely to grow rather than shrink based on these factors.

Additional drivers that have impacted market potential over time include technology and alternative delivery methods. Smartphones have eliminated the need for a stand-alone MP3 player and streaming services like Spotify and Pandora have eliminated the need to buy the music.

A good use of market drivers is to build a predictive model of your market. You can then monitor the drivers for changes and test the model for its effectiveness in predicting the market. This isn't necessarily to predict actual sales, but to watch for major shifts in either the drivers or the underlying mechanics of the market so you can react and make sound decisions more quickly. Even where the data to build a true predictive model are not available, the thought exercise can be quite revealing.

Value Mapping

Many companies spend a lot of time evaluating and managing their supply chain. A supply chain typically focuses on the network of suppliers and channel partners required to produce and deliver an offering. It is entirely different to focus on a value chain or value map.

A value map looks downstream to understand the dynamics and economics of delivering your solution to an end user, and it goes as far downstream as you can reasonably get. If you sell plastic that's used to make car door handles, the value map ends at the occupant of the car using the door handle. It then works back through all the steps to provide that solution until it gets to you. The fundamental goal of this exercise is to identify and understand your customer.

Asking, "Who is my customer?" is a seemingly simple, but often deceptively difficult question to answer. And in most B2B markets, the answer is typically a combination of, "It depends on why you are asking" and "There are several different customers."

Why such vague answers? Because B2B value chains are rarely simple. They typically involve multiple companies and a complex, multi-step network to solve end user problems.

Ignoring this complexity can be deadly. For example, part of Nest's success in thermostats may have been possible because the existing competitors focused more on distributors and contractors, often forgetting the end customer. We think it certainly played a role.

There are often consultants, engineers, regulators, value-added resellers, service providers, distributors, installers, suppliers of other components, and a host of others that can impact the buying decision. And often, the person or entity receiving the value has little or no connection to the person making the purchase decision. So in order to build an effective strategy, you first need to understand the players and dynamics of the market.

There are three components to a value map analysis: product flow, decision flow, and profit flow. If you don't evaluate all three, you may miss opportunities and/or threats to your strategy.

Product Flow

Product flow is the most obvious component. Who touches your product on its way to delivering an outcome for the end customer? Who is required to stock it, deliver it, install it, integrate it, and maintain it throughout its entire lifecycle? This is typically the easiest part of the value map.

Decision Flow

A value map needs to illustrate the decision flow. Who is involved in making the buying decision? Who influences the buying decision? Who regulates what can be done? Who specifies how the solution should work and what should go into it? Who can block the decision? Who determines when and how the solution is used?

This aspect of the value map can be difficult. A simple, transactional purchase may have one primary decision maker, but there are often many more players in the decision-making process.

A regulator, for instance, may never buy your offering, but they can certainly impact your ability to sell it by creating a rule that requires hearing protection for noise above 80dB and your "silent hammer" generates 90dB of noise. And an end-user, like the ironworker wearing your company's safety harness, may not be involved in the purchase decisions, but HOW he or she uses the harness has a big impact on the value they receive.

In short, recognize the need to understand every role and every entity in your market that can impact the decision-making process.

Profit Flow

Profit flow is arguably the most difficult part of a value map because it requires a deep understanding of the economics at every step in the market. How do each of the players make money? How much money do they make, both as a percentage of their price and by the total available profit they capture?

Let's illustrate the difference. Our client had a very profitable business selling components that were a critical part of the fire and security systems for commercial buildings. This client was selling about $200 worth of product per job, at gross margins approaching 60%. Sounds pretty good, right?

Not when you consider that those $200 components go into a system that costs the end customer about $6,000, with the system manufacturer making a 30% margin. The system requires professional installation costing $10,000, with the installer having a 15% profit margin.

Finally, the systems are almost always monitored by a service provider that charges $3,000/year for an average of 10 years and has a 10% profit margin.

Thus, the component manufacturer has a $120 profit margin on a system that costs the customer $40,000 and that generates over $6,300 of margin for others in the value chain. Our customer was capturing less than 2% of the total value created, even though they provided a critical component in the entire system.

Another example of the power of a value chain analysis involves a material with many different end-use applications that is sold through multi-step distribution. One application was as an additive for a consumer product. The material had a direct impact on the performance of the end-product and was better than any other material on the market.

In analyzing the value-map, here is what our client found:

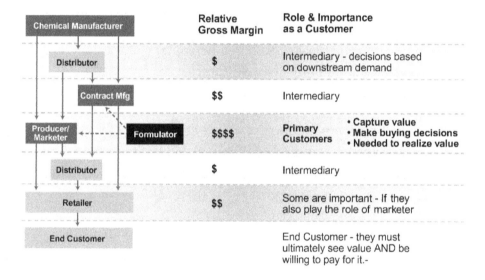

In this particular market, there is often a formulator that is typically a lone-wolf who develops a recipe for making a high-quality product. They then license their formula to manufacturers and charge a royalty for every product shipped. They never purchase any meaningful quantity of ingredients, typically just asking distributors for small samples of different materials so they can experiment until they find the best recipe.

If you look at the value chain purely from the perspective of product flow, the formulator is invisible. On the other hand, if you look at it from the decision process and even more so from the profit perspective, the formulator is the most important customer in the entire value chain. They both specify what goes into the product, and they are in the position to capture the largest share of the value created.

Be sure to do a value chain analysis before launching a new offering. In addition to understanding how your product flows, make sure you know who's involved in the decision-making process, who influences the process, and how the economics work at all levels of the market. This may not always produce startling insights, but it is a necessary foundation for the critical steps ahead.

Summary

When you are defining your market, keep in mind that it's about the customer, not you. Define it from the perspective of your customers' problem, not from a product perspective.

There is almost always room for growth if, as part of defining your market, you look at:

- The problem you're solving

- How you can solve that problem in different ways

- For whom you are solving the problem

- How you deliver the solution to the problem

Always remember that economics, which we talk about next in Chapter 4 (Microeconomics: A Digression), is the best tool for understanding potential market opportunities. Microeconomics is critical to understanding why the value chain is structured as it is, who makes money, and why.

4

Microeconomics: A Digression

Microeconomics in a strategy book? You're kidding, right? No, but we understand your reaction.

One of the authors distinctly remembers his first interview with a big consulting firm. He tried to hide his surprise when the partner interviewing him said that their strategy work was "basically applied microeconomics." It probably didn't show on his face, but his brain was spinning. He was part-way through his MBA program and had recently taken courses in strategy and microeconomics. It never occurred to him that they had anything to do with each other.

Microeconomics was all about confusing terminology, graphs, slopes, and intercepts. Strategy, on the other hand, was touchy-feely discussions of market forces and trends that, usually with the benefit of hindsight, explained why some companies fared better than others.

Here's how we have reconciled the two and why we believe it is absolutely essential to include a refresher on microeconomics in our book about strategy.

The Basics

At its most fundamental level, microeconomics tells us that when products or services are commodities and markets display perfect competition, company profits tend toward ordinary returns. This means just enough money to cover your costs plus the cost of capital and no more. There's nothing left to pay for better marketing or more R&D to find the next great idea. There's not even enough money to pay for this book.

And remember that when economists say "commodity" they mean a product or service that is not differentiated, not just goods bought and sold on a trading floor.

Further, if your product is not a commodity today, it is almost certainly trending that way. Unless you operate in a heavily regulated market, good ideas get copied and the copies get better over time. That's what market competition does and why we benefit from competition as consumers.

The computer industry is a great example of prices declining over time. The cost of computing power dropped by a factor of 100 million from 1980 to 2010 (Nordhaus, 2007). The following chart shows the approximate cost of one billion instructions per second (BIPS) of processing on a logarithmic scale.

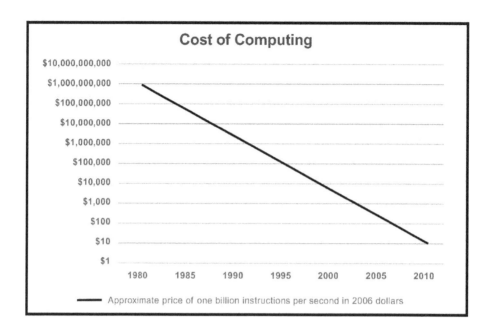

Cost of Computing

Approximate price of one billion instructions per second in 2006 dollars

If the goal of strategy is to improve profit, then strategy must avoid commoditization by finding and sustaining ways to differentiate. And since good ideas are copied by your competitors, albeit imperfectly and over time, the need for good strategy never goes away. You cannot rest on the great invention of the previous management team. As some of our clients in the chemical industry discovered the hard way, yesterday's specialty is today's commodity.

The bottom line is that if you can't articulate your differentiation in a very realistic way, you are probably well along the path to commoditization. By default, the only strategy left in a true commodity market is to win the "race to the bottom." There will eventually be a period of over-capacity followed by the resulting price war where the only way to win is to be the lowest cost producer.

Thinking in Economic Terms

In our consulting practice, when we began defining our work in Grassroots Strategy using economic terms, we discovered that many people are not naturally economic thinkers. They were as confused as the author when interviewing with that consulting firm. In particular, we noticed this most frequently when we listened to their answers to "why" questions.

When asked why a potential customer did not buy from them, salespeople might respond, "Well, that customer is stupid," or slightly more politely, "That customer just doesn't understand our value." These explanations may be satisfying at the bar when licking your wounds after a lost sale, and they may even be partially true, but they do not represent good microeconomic thinking.

Explanations that present the customer's psychological and emotional conditions as the reason for their decision cannot be tested. Nor are they helpful if the goal is to change the next customer's decision. That's the problem with non-economic thinking. The real reason for asking why the customer didn't buy from you is to uncover what you have to change in order to change the customer's decision. It goes without saying that "the customer is stupid" is not something you can change.

Here is a somewhat contrived example. Imagine you work for a European automobile manufacturer and want to sell your small cars in the US. Early in your market research you realize that, on average, cars are bigger in the US than they are in Europe. More later on the dangers of thinking in terms of averages.

When your boss asks about this phenomenon, you might be tempted to reply, "Americans just love their big cars." This undoubtedly has an element of truth to it, and you could no doubt provide research into the attitudes of SUV (sport utility vehicle) owners that would support it. But if your goal is to sell small cars to Americans, that answer is not helpful because it is not a microeconomic answer.

The most obvious economic explanation is the difference in gasoline prices. As of this writing, gasoline prices are two to three times higher in most of Europe than in the US. We now have a testable hypothesis: Americans would buy smaller cars if they paid higher gasoline prices.

In fact, the US ran that test in early 2008 when the price of oil increased by over 100% in less than a year (USEIA, n.d.). Sales of the very largest class of SUVs fell by over 35% in 2008 and by over 34% in 2009 (Cain, 2014).

Interestingly, sales did not fall to zero, as apparently some Americans really do love their big cars. And SUV sales started to bounce back even before gasoline prices started to fall again, so other factors may be at work. But, we cannot reject the hypothesis that higher gasoline prices explain at least some of the difference in vehicle size between the US and Europe.

Microeconomics asks us to look at the trade-offs customers make. Why might Americans and Europeans have different trade-offs when it comes to car buying? Beyond the difference in gasoline prices, here's a partial list of potential explanations:

- Americans have larger families and are willing to pay more, both upfront and in operating costs, to have more room in their vehicles. Anyone who has ever driven with two or three children in car seats can probably relate.

- Americans tend to have longer commutes and spend more time in their cars, in part because many areas have fewer public transportation options. They might spend more for comfort and possibly safety since there are so many other SUVs on the road. This is a perverse sort of "network economics" where the value of something increases the more other people use it.

- Europe does not have a big car-friendly infrastructure. Regardless of gas prices, you would never find a place to park if you drove a big American SUV in Paris or Milan.

While these explanations (or hypotheses) are far from complete, they do pass our test of good economic thinking. They evaluate the trade-offs made by consumers when selecting a vehicle, and they state these perspectives in ways that are testable. We can change the input variables and see how it changes customer choices.

And yet, most of these hypotheses are still not very helpful, even though they are significantly more insightful than our original non-economic explanations. We could lobby the US government for better public transportation or higher gasoline taxes (and make a lot of enemies in the process), but we cannot directly change these background variables ourselves.

If we ignore the averages and drill into the details of individual customer groups, we might uncover pockets of consumers that would make different trade-offs, such as young, childless drivers in urban markets with good public transportation. More on this approach in Chapter 6 (Segmentation).

It is interesting to note that when Fiat launched the subcompact Fiat 500 in the US, it was positioned primarily as being "fun to drive," not as fuel efficient or more economical to operate. Perhaps their initial success was evidence of an overlooked or underserved segment among younger car buyers.

Note that when we say that microeconomic thinking is the best way to explain customer behavior, we are not saying people only care about money or short-term financial results. The field of behavioral economics gives us lots of examples where people will act against their short-term financial interest to serve some broader purpose. For example, people will give up short term gains in a profit-sharing game in order to teach an opponent a lesson.

We include these attributes when we define value. If the customer is willing to pay more for using the industry standard so they fit in with their peers, then we can incorporate that into our understanding of value. For a good overview of behavioral economics, we suggest *Misbehaving: The Making of Behavioral Economics* by Richard Thaler, who is often called the father of behavioral economics.

Defining Microeconomics

Few definitions of microeconomics are fully satisfying to us, so here is our definition synthesized from multiple sources:

> **Microeconomics** is the science dedicated to understanding how individuals and companies make choices among scarce resources.

Let's explore this definition in more detail. Microeconomics is a science, meaning it uses the same scientific method you learned in middle school. Applying scientific method allows us to observe something about the world, form a hypothesis as to why it happens that way, and then design an experiment to test the hypothesis.

In our car example, we could easily test what happens when retail gasoline prices rise. Even if we cannot change gasoline prices unilaterally, we can test this hypothesis over time using event studies or geographical cross-sections. In both cases, we need to hold all other factors constant. Several studies have done just that and confirm that retail gasoline prices predict some, but not all, of the differences in average car size (Leard & Linn, 2016).

Microeconomics vs. Macroeconomics

Notice that our definition is for microeconomics and not macroeconomics. The key difference is that microeconomics deals with the interaction among businesses and between businesses and their customers, while macroeconomics deals with issues at the country level and the interaction among countries. Most of what you hear economists opining about on television is macroeconomics.

So how does macroeconomics jive with testing hypotheses and exploring the trade-offs that are essential to building a grassroots strategy? It doesn't. The essence of something being a science is the repeatable experiment. With macroeconomics, the experiment is generally run just once, and with no control group.

For example, the Fed may or may not raise interest rates next quarter but whatever they do, they cannot go back in time and run an experiment to see what would happen if they made a different choice. Macroeconomists argue all the time for the same reason as sports talk show hosts: no one knows what would have happened had they left that starting pitcher in for one more inning, and no one can go back and replay the game, so they are free to speculate.

Because macroeconomists deal with issues of national interest, they get a lot more airtime than microeconomists. Microeconomists also tend to agree a lot, which makes for boring television. In fact, about 98% of practicing microeconomists would agree on the following four premises:

- Every decision is a trade-off; there are no "non-economic" decisions

- The best measure of value is what someone is willing to pay

- People think "on the margin"

- People respond to incentives

This last premise is so fundamental that some microeconomists don't think it even needs to be on the list!

Let's discuss these premises in turn, because their implications for good strategic thinking are important.

Every Decision is a Trade-Off

This premise pertains to customer needs. These needs mean something different than when your kid says, "I need that new video game." This typically translates to, "I really want you to buy that for me." Makes sense coming from your kid but as input from a customer, it's not particularly helpful.

By our definition, a need is a want combined with a willingness to pay. So, it is not enough to list the things your customers want. You must strive to understand the trade-offs they are willing to make among these wants. In other words, how much of something else are they willing to give up to get the attribute they want more? Another way to say this is understanding your customers' economics. If you're paying attention, your job just got harder. More on how to do this in Chapter 5 (Customer Value).

We once worked with a polymer company whose marketing team insisted they understood their customers' needs. To prove it, they produced a list of eleven attributes their customers valued: impact resistance, temperature resistance, UV stability, etc. They thought their job was finished when they handed this list over to R&D.

While happy to have the input, the R&D team understood immediately that it was insufficient. They understood that there were technical trade-offs making it nearly impossible to produce a polymer compound that improved all eleven attributes at once. Making some attributes better would only be possible by making other attributes worse. After much good effort, they came up with a formulation that improved seven attributes but made four worse.

Rather than wait and see if anyone bought it (spoiler alert: no one did), wouldn't it have been better if the marketing team understood the relative value of these attributes for different customer groups (segmentation) and worked with R&D to design unique offerings that specifically met their needs? Yes, but this requires economics: matching the financial trade-offs customers face with the very real technical trade-offs faced in the lab. Scientists and engineers understand trade-offs. This is why people with technical backgrounds are some of our favorite students.

The Best Measure of Value is What You're Willing to Pay

This premise is so important that we devote all of Chapter 5 (Customer Value) to it. It bears repeating because so many companies confuse value and cost. But the difference is clear: cost is from our perspective; value is from the customers' perspective.

Let's demonstrate this using a bottle of water. The production cost is well-known by the company that produced it, and there is likely a cost accountant within the company who knows that cost to within a hundredth of a cent given its size, plant, etc. But what is the value of that bottle of water?

Value is defined as willingness to pay, so we can say its value is at least 25 cents when purchased by the case at a warehouse club. Its value is at least $2.99 at the airport gift shop and at least $7.00 at a concert or sporting event. Note that we say "at least" because as long as we observe people paying those prices, we know the value is more than that, at least to those who paid that price.

Here is an extreme example. You're stuck on a desert island with a single bottle of water that has to last until you are rescued. What is its value then? Slightly less extreme is being in a hotel in Shanghai where the first bottle of water is free and additional bottles cost 80 RMB (about $13 US at the time).

If the next best alternative is being sick during your entire trip because you drank tap water, some might consider it. But as we will see below, prices are also incentives.

So, the high price of the second bottle could inspire someone (like one of the authors) to walk to the convenience store across the street where the same bottle is sold for 10 RMB, even if this meant putting his pants back on and dodging Shanghai traffic.

Be careful not to project your beliefs onto the customer. Too often we hear things like, "Well, we know that our product is better." Even if you can produce test results that your performance is better along some dimension, that performance difference is irrelevant unless it creates value for the customer.

We vividly remember a client that poured millions of dollars into R&D to improve the durability of a safety system. Sadly, they discovered that customers only bought safety systems because regulations required them to. Since they hoped they would never actually use it, they always bought the least expensive system that met the regulations, regardless of its projected durability.

The flipside may also be true. Perceived value on which customers base their buying decisions may be greater than actual value, and not just in consumer marketing. For example, your product performs well in other applications, so a customer may assume it will work well in a new application.

But as we will discuss later, B2B customers are continuously adjusting their perceptions and can quickly change them if performance does not match their expectations.

People Think "On the Margin"

Most companies are set up to report averages: average cost, average price, etc. But customers decide on the margin: the price vs. value to me relative to my options at the time. This is potentially one of the most difficult microeconomic concepts to internalize. It is very hard to imagine the "marginal customer" because you are rarely that customer.

Imagine a scenario where Starbucks raises the price of a cup of coffee by 10%. (Okay, that may not be so hard to imagine). What will happen to their sales? Economics dictates that an increase in price will be offset by a decrease in demand, and what is true in total must have an impact on the margin. But, can you really imagine someone walking out of Starbucks without buying a grande latte because the price increased from $3.90 to $4.29? Not likely but remember, you are not the customer.

Very often in consumer businesses, the marginal customers are what's known as "super users." These super users don't buy one latte a day, but four or more. If their latte habit suddenly causes them to break a second $20 bill one day, they may decide that four lattes a day is enough. That's why it's so hard to understand the marginal customer, as it may be that customer's tastes and trade-offs look nothing like yours.

People Respond to Incentives

To this premise we like to add, "…but not always in the way we thought they would." Let's explain. To an economist, a price is an incentive. If beef prices are high, people are motivated to eat less beef and presumably eat more chicken or tofu. This is what makes microeconomics so fascinating and so powerful.

Millions of consumers, most of whom never studied economics and nearly none of whom are drawing demand curves and calculating cross-elasticities for chicken and beef, are making individual decisions that, in aggregate, are predictable!

The business lesson is that when you change your price, you are changing your customers' incentive. Raising prices may seem attractive in the short term but in reality, you are creating more incentive for your customers to use less of your product or work harder to find substitutes.

There is a story from the aerospace industry that is particularly instructive. Aircraft wheels and brakes are a complex and durable system that must absorb the impact of an aircraft landing and then help the plane come to a stop shortly thereafter.

About twenty years ago, material technology had evolved so that the brake rotors could be made from carbon fiber rather than steel.

This resulted in significant weight savings because there are multiple rotors per wheel and many wheels on a large aircraft.

Airlines were very interested in the weight savings, as brakes are used only on the ground and they are dead weight while the plane is in the air. But the airlines were capital constrained and could neither afford to take planes out of service nor pay to upgrade their brakes.

Then someone had the brilliant idea of making brakes a variable cost. This was not long after General Electric began charging for their aircraft engines, not as a capital purchase, but as a variable operating expense using Power by the Hour. One of the aircraft brake companies thought they could combine the expected inspection, maintenance, and replacement costs with an embedded financing charge and bundle them into a "per use" price.

Since the primary use of aircraft brakes is to bring a plane to a stop after landing, they chose price per landing. And since the aerospace industry loves acronyms, at least one of the brake manufacturers called it Cost per Aircraft Landing, or CPAL (Adams, 2013).

According to the folks we spoke with, the program was initially quite successful. With no up-front cost, the airlines could take immediate advantage of the weight savings and subsequent fuel savings. And their risk was reduced as well. If a plane was not flying, they were not paying for the brakes. But the program had one major drawback. In changing the way they priced, they changed the airlines' incentives.

It turns out that there are three different devices that are used in varying proportions (Kampf, 2016) to stop a plane after it lands: the brakes on the wheels, the spoilers, and the reverse thrusters on the engines. By making the brakes a fixed cost per landing, the airlines incurred no additional cost for excess wear due to heavy usage.

Conversely, if they used the reverse thrusters, the airlines paid for the additional fuel burned and extra wear on the engines. So rumor has it that pilots in many commercial airlines were instructed to use the brakes first and only use the reverse thrusters on short runways or where required for safety reasons.

Did the engineers who developed the initial cost projections anticipate this change in pilot behavior? If not, one can be certain that actual maintenance costs were significantly higher than what they predicted. It is safe to assume that if that happened, it would dramatically impact the profitability of the business. And since others in the aerospace brake business had adopted this way of pricing and airlines had come to expect to pay as a variable cost, it would be difficult to change back.

How could they get this wrong? In short, by failing to think about economics.

One would assume that their initial cost calculations were correct, but they likely assumed no change in the operating procedures and corresponding maintenance costs. Unfortunately, that was a bad assumption because by changing the trade-offs their customers faced, they changed their decisions. This could have been predicted just as grocery shoppers would buy more chicken if the price of beef doubles.

Economics is Common Sense

Many of these rules come down to common sense. Is anyone surprised, for example, that incentives change behavior? Yet bad economic thinking abounds in corporations. Is common sense really that uncommon? Apparently. Here's our view of this why this is the case and what you can do to change it.

To begin, we believe that economics is taught poorly at many colleges and universities. Or perhaps it is taught extraordinarily well, but it is wasted on an audience of college sophomores whose minds are elsewhere. But if you are like us, and you only had one undergraduate overview course in economics, it probably covered both micro- and macroeconomics and was enough to make your head spin.

For those who were good at math, the chapters on microeconomics were fun. You drew charts and calculated intercepts. There was one right answer that you could find with a formula and you could check your answer. Engineering-type students were right at home with microeconomics.

Macroeconomics was just the opposite and had no straight, easily calculated answer. Every theory had an "on the other hand" provision, as in "a strong dollar is really good but on the other hand, a strong dollar can be really bad." When faced with conflicting recommendations from his economic advisors, a very frustrated President Harry Truman is said to have commented, "What I really need is a good one-handed economist."

Not surprisingly, the students who excelled in macroeconomics were liberal arts majors who could write a great paper taking both sides of an issue. An important skill, but not helpful in predicting customer behavior.

In part because economics is so poorly understood, we are also bombarded with bad economic thinking from popular media. Journalists in the US are taught to write using something called the "volitional narrative." Volition is an act of will, so the logic of a volitional narrative says something bad happened, find the bad person who wanted it to happen.

This may be sufficient when reporting that eight school buses were vandalized and police are questioning local gang members. But this logic doesn't work when reporting complex news about the economy.

For example, if you get your news about the economy from popular outlets that are designed to give you a 30-second sound bite, you might have been led to believe that the financial crisis of 2008 was caused by greedy bankers. Greed was certainly a contributing factor, but since greed has been around long before the advent of modern banking, it's hard to say it was the primary cause. As one commentator observed at the time, "Blaming the financial crisis on greed is like blaming a plane crash on gravity."

What did cause the financial collapse? We won't attempt to cover all possible explanations here. Clearly, the dynamics combined complex and interacting regulations from various government and rating agencies, and banks who were making so much money that they had powerful incentives to overlook warning signs. This was probably exacerbated by a healthy dose of group think.

Too many companies make similar mistakes when attributing their business results. They too are faced with complex and interrelated causes: market conditions, customer trends, competitor tactics, and their own initiatives. When business units have a great year, the success is too often attributed to the business leaders being "really smart people." When the same business performs poorly the following year, did its leaders suddenly become "dumb?"

Accountant or Economist?

With few exceptions, practicing good economic thinking is difficult for most corporations because they think like accountants, not economists. Clearly, good accounting is critically important for knowing where we make money and paying the taxes we owe to stay out of jail.

But accounting has nothing to say about predicting the future; it's all about explaining the past. Economics is about making "what if" predictions such as, "If we raised prices 10%, how much less would customers buy?" Accounting is silent on this topic.

The problem persists because accountants have traditionally defined the language we use to talk about our businesses. An example is using the word "accretive" as if it explains some real economic phenomenon. Accretive simply means that percentage profit margins went up so if we own an 8% profit business and acquire a 12% profit business, it is accretive. But this tells us very little about whether it was a good idea.

The same is true of another accounting favorite, "margin dilution." Margins do not dilute themselves. Margins go down because prices dropped or costs rose. Asking "why?" and "what can we change to reverse it?" are questions for economists, not accountants.

Here's a practical application of this dilemma. Your business is developing costing for a new customer or initiative. Accountants can tell you your average cost, probably to the penny, but it's inappropriate to use the average cost for analyzing a specific initiative. Economists will tell you that the right cost is your "marginal cost." This is the cost of making one more unit, or the cost of serving one more customer.

Except your marginal cost is not found on your income statement. If you are running below capacity and there are no incremental fixed costs associated with taking one more order, then your marginal cost is close to your variable cost. But even that may not be easy to find on your income statement.

Cost of Goods Sold (COGS) tends to have both variable costs and allocated fixed costs. If these fixed costs are really fixed (you wouldn't hire an extra supervisor at the plant just to process one more order), then they are not part of your marginal cost.

The flip side is that your marginal cost should include "cost to serve." These are the incremental costs associated with processing that additional order or servicing that additional customer. Again, these are not directly found on the income statement. Most tend to show up in overhead or Selling, General, and Administrative costs (SG&A). Cost to serve may be low if a customer can be served online and buys standard products at standard terms. Or it may be very high if it requires opening a sales office in a new region, or requires product or service customization or support.

If this sounds difficult, it can be. But it's critical that you begin thinking like an economist. Thinking like an accountant can lead to decisions that are precise, but absolutely wrong.

Economics and Grassroots Strategy

We have heard many statements over the years that do not reflect good economic thinking, and have presented a quick graduate level course to address this shortcoming. Here is the final exam. Can you identify what's wrong with these statements from an economic thinking perspective?

1. We can't afford to bid on that business because it will dilute our margins.

2. We have been losing business because our competitors are pricing irrationally and our customers are stupid.

3. We can't invest to win that business because of our capital constraints (or head count freeze, or asset turns target, or fixed engineering budget, or ...).

4. We need to enter this market because it is fragmented, growing, and has high margins. What else is there to know?

You've probably figured out that none of these statements reflects good microeconomic thinking. Here are some insights into why not.

1. **We can't afford to bid on that business because it will dilute our margins.**

   Remember, margin dilution is an accounting term, not an economic term. It is technically true that if your current business operates at 12% profit and you are considering a big order at 11%, your profit percentage will go down. But if that new order is truly incremental business and it is big enough, it might be a great business decision.

   The bottom line is that you take dollars, not percentage points, to the bank, even if accountants (or those who write our incentive goals) sometimes forget this fact.

2. **We have been losing business because our competitors are pricing irrationally, and our customers are stupid.**

   This statement actually comes from the client making the safety equipment described earlier in this chapter. The customer wasn't stupid; they were buying this piece of equipment because it was a regulatory requirement and they hoped to never actually use it. So, while our client's equipment was more durable and reliable, those attributes created no value.

Similarly, competitors knew that they could not compete with our client on features, but they had a huge cost advantage largely because their product was not over-engineered. Was competing on price irrational? The sad epilogue is that the client had to lose three big orders before they finally started asking the right questions and getting to the economic "why" behind their satisfying, but not helpful reasons.

3. **We can't invest to win that business because of our capital constraints (or head count freeze, or asset turns target, or fixed engineering budget, or...).**

This one is a little tricky. Unless you are a CEO or an owner, you need to live with these constraints or risk losing your job. However, it's important to remember that these constraints or targets were set without perfect knowledge of how the year would unfold and what opportunities might be available. As important as they are, these metrics are not as important as the ultimate metric: profit.

Here's an example to highlight how we suggest you think about this.

Our client that manufactures components for the aerospace industry discovered an opportunity to sell more spare parts in relatively remote parts of the world where there was a willingness to pay for genuine, OEM-certified parts, but often none were available. They estimated a potential $20M in incremental sales at gross margins of 70% to 80%. But achieving this would require adding inventory in these locations and because of the low volumes, that inventory would turn relatively slowly.

The team was reluctant to present their idea to management because one of their business unit goals that year was reducing working capital, and adding inventory would work in the opposite direction. Here is how we encouraged them.

As a shareholder, do you want this additional profit? Absolutely! As the board that represents shareholders, do you want this? Clearly, Yes! As the CEO who reports to the board, do you want to do this? Yes, of course! The challenge was to find someone on the org chart positioned between the team and the CEO with the authority to adjust the working capital target or reallocate the targeted reduction to other parts of the business.

Our counsel was to approach that person respectfully and thoughtfully, and base the case for change on real market data. With a little creativity, it may be possible to persuade companies to make the better economic move, even if other metrics discourage it.

4. **We need to enter this market because it is fragmented, growing, and has high margins. What else is there to know?**

This is precisely the argument we reviewed in Chapter 3 (Opportunity and Market Definition) relative to the retail jewelry market. Although we preach market-back thinking, that doesn't mean looking **only** at the market. Key questions include, "Is this a good market for us?' and "Can we bring differentiation that will allow us to win?"

In Chapter 7 (Value Proposition), we refer to these as our "right to play" and "right to win." The key is the economic logic in your thinking, not just gathering more data on the market as it exists today.

Summary

We can wrap up this very important digression by revisiting our assertion that economic thinking is really common sense. You just need to practice it at work as you would in other parts of your life.

Using our last example, suppose your neighbor knocked on your door one evening with a tempting proposition. "Hey! Give me $100,000 and you can be my partner in a new jewelry store." Before you whip out your checkbook, we hope you ask some common-sense questions. "What do you know about running a jewelry store?" addresses the right to play. "What's going to make your store more successful than the jewelry stores in town that go out of business every year?" addresses the right to win.

We hope you are on board with the importance of microeconomic thinking. In our experience, it is the foundation for understanding customer value and applying that understanding to make practical decisions about customer targets, product features, and price. This is the logic underpinning grassroots strategy.

Customer Value

Many companies talk about the value they deliver to customers, but few actually quantify that value and articulate how it will manifest into better business performance.

Talk of value is typically followed by lists of features, functions, attributes, and properties. It's amazing how many sales brochures, presentations, and websites focus exclusively on the features of the product. After reviewing a client's messaging, a colleague commented, "It's all about you, baby. Where is the customer in all this?"

A deeper understanding of customer value will help your entire organization focus on meeting customer needs in a way that differentiates your offering and helps them make more money. That's the basis of a winning strategy.

Defining Customer Value

Let's start with our definition of value (Gross, n.d.):

> Value is the **hypothetical price** for your **total offering** at which a particular **customer** would be at **economic break-even** relative to their **next best alternative**.

Now let's deconstruct this definition by discussing its key components in a slightly different order.

- The **total offering** includes everything that you provide for the customer, which means it goes far beyond the actual product or service. It includes support, terms, delivery, responsiveness, and anything else that could impact the value received by the customer, whether they are written into a sales contract or merely understood.

- Every **customer** has a unique set of needs and will therefore value different aspects of your offering in different ways. Later, when we discuss segmentation, hopefully we will find groups of customers with similar sets of needs that will value things in a similar way. For now, let's assume that each customer is unique.

- The value you deliver to a customer is not absolute. The customer's **next best alternative** is always the relevant comparison. The next best alternative is whatever else a customer could do to solve their problem. This could include building an in-house solution, buying from a competitor, or continuing to do what they're already doing.

  We'll talk more about this later but for now, understand that your customer is always evaluating alternatives when assessing the value that you create for them.

- The **hypothetical price** where the customer is at **economic break-even** is our final consideration. Overall, this means value is measured in the same units as price using a form of currency. Although it can be difficult to calculate exactly when a customer is at economic break-even, it is extremely important that you at least try to estimate that point.

  If you charge one cent more than their break-even point, they are better off going with the alternative. And if you charge anything less, they are better off buying from you. Although you can never estimate that price exactly because you will never have perfect information, the more you understand it, the better you can target the right customers and set the best prices. You will rarely be able to charge this hypothetical maximum price, but you will be better equipped to set prices that align with your value.

This definition of customer value contains what we consider three fundamental truths.

Customer Value is Always:

- Customer specific
- Measured in currency
- Relative to their next best alternative

We've talked about how value is customer specific and relative to the next best alternative, but we haven't said much about why value must be measured in currency. In a B2B world, it's all about the bottom line. If you can't improve a customer's bottom line, there's no reason for them to buy from you. And if you can't measure value in currency, you can't know if and by how much you are impacting their bottom line.

Customers don't care about your brand, service, quality, reliability, per se. They care about how those attributes impact their business.

A colleague spent much of his career working at an ad agency whose clients included several major consumer brands. He decided to leave consumer advertising when he realized that if you dig deep enough into consumer motivations, it always comes down to attracting a mate (it turns out that sex really does sell). Eventually he tired of trying to persuade people that this new product would make them more desirable in some way. What he enjoys most about B2B marketing is that you are selling money. If you can help your customers make more money, then you can charge more. Period.

Of course, no customer will ever request that you raise their prices. That is why developing objective insights into value from the customer's perspective is so critical.

Customer Value Traps

Here are some potential traps to avoid when it comes to understanding customer value in a B2B environment:

Customer Value Traps

1. Thinking your brand creates value
2. Focusing on "ity" words
3. Trying to trick customers
4. Believing value is absolute and timeless
5. Focusing on the wrong next-best alternative
6. Thinking that "the best" always creates more value

Trap 1: Thinking your Brand Creates Value by Itself

In B2B, as in B2C, your brand is a proxy for your customers' expectations based on their and others' experiences. But rarely do your customers associate personal attributes with your brand as they might a consumer brand. Therefore, in B2B, it is not the brand, in and of itself, that creates value. Trying to create a brand without something tangible to back it up is extremely difficult in B2B. Or worse, if your customers have had a negative experience with your company, spending money on a "branding" campaign could strengthen the link between that negative experience and your brand.

B2B customers care about what they will receive in return for buying your offering. This expectation is your brand promise, and you often have to dig deep to understand what that means to your customer. Does it mean you will always be there to help them when they have a problem? Does it mean you will always ship on time? Does it mean that your product never fails? Or does it mean that you over-promise and then don't answer the phone when they call tech support? Their impressions are your brand reality.

Even if experience suggests that customers will pay a premium for your brand, you need to keep digging. If you stop there and don't truly understand what that brand means to your customer, you are sitting on a ticking time bomb. The only way out is to understand the value of the entire customer experience from their perspective.

Trap 2: Focusing on "ity" Words

We often work with clients who believe their customers will pay a premium because they have the best quality, reliability, durability, compatibility, connectivity, etc., in the market. We call these "ity" words, and they are little more than adjectives with the "ity" suffix.

Our job is to challenge the belief that "ity" words are a good way to describe value.

Let's use quality as an example. When communicating your value, quality doesn't mean the same thing to all customers because quality is subjective. It may well be that a Toyota is a high-quality car because you never have to take it to a mechanic to be repaired.

But it may also be that a BMW is a high-quality car because it is, as they say, "the ultimate driving machine." In each case, the customer gets to define what quality means. And in this example, there are different definitions for different customers, resulting in dramatically different prices.

Or, say you sell a measurement device. You could say it's the highest quality device on the market because it's so reliable. It will last 50 years and require no repairs. But to a customer who only needs a device to last three years, longevity beyond three years holds little additional value.

Conversely, a device lasting 50 years is important to a customer who wants to use it in a satellite that will operate for the next 30 years and cannot fail. That's a clear case where you're providing value.

Alternatively, you could also say this device is the highest quality because it measures to 0.001 percent accuracy. But to a customer who only needs one percent accuracy, 0.001 percent has no additional value over a device that delivers their needed accuracy.

Relevant here is a Six Sigma concept called the "5 Whys" that can help reveal a root cause or reason. When a sales rep asserts that his product offers the highest quality in the market, the customer will (or should) ask a series of "why" questions, such as:

- Why would I want to buy your device?
  Because the device will last 50 years.

- Why do I care that the device will last 50 years?
  Because you will have fewer failures downstream.

- Why do I care that I will have fewer failures?
  Because eventually you will have to pay maintenance and service costs, and our device will save you those costs.

The idea here is that you need to continue to ask "why" until you get to the root of the customer's needs. That's where value lies, and it's specific to each customer.

Trap 3: Trying to Trick Customers

Both of us started our careers as engineers, where there is a long-standing perception that going into marketing is like going over to "the dark side." Many people think marketing is about trying to influence people to do, buy, or believe whatever you want them to, regardless of whether it is actually good for them.

In consumer marketing, this may work in the short term. Who knew we needed a pet rock or that using a knight to pitch beer would increase market share? But most B2B customers are too sophisticated to be tricked for long. They also have the built-in protection of a procurement process and the purchasing department, which makes it harder to trick anyone even in the short term.

A good strategy, and by extension good marketing, isn't about tricking anyone. It's about figuring out your customers' problems and how you can uniquely solve them. Value must be grounded in what we would truly believe to be true if we were in the customers' shoes, not the slogans that we wish to be true.

Trap 4: Believing Value is Absolute and Timeless

Value is **always** relative to your customer's next best alternative. We talk to clients all the time who say things like, "We create $1.5 million of value, and our customers just don't recognize that." It seems logical that the value created should justify the price. But many sellers measure value in absolute vs. relative terms, and customers don't think in absolutes.

Customers are always comparing your offering to their next best alternative. It's not enough to compare and justify your value against the customer's current situation. If you don't offer more value relative to their other options, now and in the future, they may be better off going with your competition.

Let's say your solution can create $1.5 million of value with an investment of $800,000. Your net value would be $700,000. And suppose an alternative solution delivers a total value of $1 million, but the investment is only $150,000. The net value would be $850,000. In this case, the customer is better off with the solution that only delivers $1 million of total value because it delivered $150,000 of incremental value relative to your solution.

Also keep in mind that customers will assess value over time, not just at a point in time. Thus, even if an offering delivers more value and is priced similarly to the competition, if your maintenance costs over time are higher, you may actually deliver less net value.

Trap 5: Focusing on the Wrong Next Best Alternative

Imagine walking into a Mercedes dealership to buy a car. You look at different models, test drive one or two, and evaluate available options. After deciding which model and specific features you're interested in, the sales rep comes back with a price.

At this point, you pull out a Hyundai ad and tell the rep you can go down the street and get this car for half the price. Do you think the rep will negotiate with you on price? Absolutely not! They will tell you to go talk to the Hyundai dealer. Why? Because they know that the next best alternative for their target customers is not a Hyundai, and that you are wasting their time.

So, why do we accept this same argument in a B2B setting? It is critical in B2B to truly understand the entire market, including competitive offerings. If we don't understand how we compare to the alternatives in the market, then it's easy to respond incorrectly. If a competitor that doesn't have your capabilities lowers their price, does that mean you need to lower yours? Maybe not, if you truly understand your value and their next best alternative.

The flip side of this is doing nothing as the next best alternative. If the problem is big enough, don't assume the customer hasn't already found a way to address it, even if their solution is neither ideal nor elegant. Also, if the prize is big enough, competitors are likely to follow quickly with their version of your solution, even if it doesn't solve the problem as well as you did. That will still quickly erode the relative value that you deliver.

It is critical that you understand the problem, what customers are doing to solve it today, and how competitors are likely to react when you launch your solution.

Trap 6: Thinking that "the Best" Always Creates More Value

A classic marketing story helps illustrate this point. Let's go back to the 1980s and revisit the battle between Betamax and VHS video technology. Younger readers will not remember the early days of videotape but at the time, it was a classic format war. Sony introduced the Betamax format while the rest of the industry standardized on the VHS format.

Expert product reviewers and many others argued that Betamax was better because it had superior sound and picture quality. But in a relatively short number of years, the market voted and overwhelmingly choose VHS over Betamax. Some contend it was because Sony was the sole supplier for Betamax and movie distributors did not like bargaining with them. But if Betamax delivered a better experience, why didn't customers choose it?

Practicality is the real reason VHS won. Because of its form factor and lower resolution video and audio, you could fit a full-length movie on one VHS tape instead of two Betamax tapes. Which is a better experience for the customer: watching an entire movie in one sitting or being interrupted to switch tapes? The market spoke and was willing to trade picture and sound quality for a single-tape experience.

In the end, the customer defines what's best, not a technical specification. If you define best solely from the perspective of engineers who think about your offering 40+ hours per week, you are almost certainly getting it wrong. Raising the dial "to eleven" doesn't create value unless a specific set of customers have a need for it to go to eleven. And even then, you need to ask "why?" enough times to understand what's really going on before someone else figures out how to make it go to twelve.

The Value Equation

In 1998 Professors James Anderson and James Narus created the Value Equation (Anderson & Narus, 1998). Although this concept has existed for over 20 years, our experience shows that very few B2B companies actually use it to understand the relative value that they deliver to customers.

$$\textbf{Value Equation}$$
$$(V_s - P_s) > (V_{nba} - P_{nba})$$

In this equation, V_s is the value that the supplier delivers, P_s is the price that the supplier charges for the offering, V_{nba} is the value that the next best alternative delivers, and P_{nba} is the price of the next best alternative. This seemingly simple equation forces all three of our core tenets of value to be true.

First, you must understand the value for a specific customer to quantify it (customer specific). Second, in order to put it into the same equation as price, it must be measured in the same units (measured in currency). And finally, the equation compares your offering to the customer's next best alternative (relative to the next best alternative).

By doing some simple algebra, this equation enables you to calculate the maximum price that a given customer should be willing to pay:

$$\textbf{Maximum Price}$$
$$P_s < P_{nba} + (V_s - V_{nba})$$

We like to call this the **Iron Law of the Marketplace**: customers will not pay more than the value they receive. You can now see why we believe that value MUST be measured in currency to be relevant.

Only by understanding how much value a customer receives from something can you actually figure out how much they should be willing to pay for it.

The good news is that this is actually achievable in B2B markets, at least within reason. A business has financial statements, and value will always show up somewhere as increased revenue, lower cost of goods sold, lower labor cost, lower energy cost, etc. In contrast, consumers rarely have financial statements and consumers more often make decisions for reasons other than financial impact.

Let's talk about some of the implications of the value equation. Most important is that your cost to deliver the offering is not part of the value equation. As far as the customer (and value equation) are concerned, it doesn't matter how much it costs you to make or deliver your solution. It only matters how much value they receive.

Nor does it matter if you have a target margin to hit, or if you invested millions of dollars to develop the offering. That's not to say that your cost doesn't matter. Your cost is critical to evaluating the margin and earnings that your offering can contribute to the business, but it has nothing to do with what customer should be willing to pay. If the value equation shows that the maximum a customer should be willing to pay is not high enough to deliver an acceptable margin, then you shouldn't be selling it.

The value equation also tells us that if you are in a market where prices are transparent and therefore similar, even a small increment of value that you can deliver will motivate the customer to buy from you. In a recent article, Jim Anderson calls taking advantage of these seemingly small value elements, "tie-breaker selling."

On the other hand, if you are in a true commodity market where there are no differences in value, then the lowest price will win. Luckily, there is almost always a way to create incremental value if you understand the customer and their needs. In our view, true commodity markets are rare.

We will work through how to identify value dimensions over the rest of this chapter. Luckily, you don't have to quantify every single way in which your offering creates value, just the differences between the value your offering delivers and the value your customer's next best alternative delivers.

However, it is important to note that sometimes the most important elements of value can come from those that are hardest to quantify like safety, confidence, etc. In Chapter 8 (Value Pricing), we will explore how to use the value equation in pricing.

The Elements of Value

When we run workshops around this concept, we ask participants to generate a long list of value elements (Anderson & Narus, 1998). Then we ask them to make sure they are worded in a way that can readily be translated into currency.

From running that exercise hundreds of times, we have compiled a list of some of the most common mistakes:

Often Mistaken for Value	Value Often Overlooked or Given Away
• Low cost • Effective promotion strategy • Broad product line • Brand • Leading technology • One-stop shopping • Bundled offering • Integrated solution	• Exclusivity or first to market • Technical service/support • Engineering or design assistance • Market access • Risk assumption • Unique perspective on trends • Continuity of supply • Assured availability or fast delivery

Let's talk through some of the elements that are often mistaken for value starting with low cost. Intuitively, it seems like being the lowest cost solution creates value. The problem is that your cost has nothing to do with the value created, and how you choose to price is your mechanism for capturing and sharing value. More about this in Chapter 8 (Value Pricing).

We often hear that having the broadest product line is a strength. A customer only cares about your broad product line if it has all of the products that solve their specific problems. Likewise with describing your products as having "leading technology" or being an "integrated solution." If you can't clearly articulate how this will make more money for your customer, then it is not a value element.

Classifying Value Elements

Brainstorming the value elements for your offering should result in a very long list. When we conduct Grassroots Strategy sessions with clients, they often come up with three to four flipchart pages of value elements.

When we tell them to quantify their value, the response is usually something like, "How in the world are we going to quantify all of those things?" Luckily, it is rare to need to quantify every value element, since value is relative to the customer's next best alternative. So before we go about quantifying the value elements, we first classify them relative to the next best alternative.

The classification process evaluates each value element based on your differentiation against that next best alternative. There are three classifications: Parity, Differentiated, and Opportunity, and variations of each.

Parity (P)

Parity (P) means that your offering is no better or worse at delivering that value element. Since value is relative, if your offering isn't better, then it doesn't create any value relative to the next best alternative. That means you don't need to quantify it because it will be $0. That's not to say that your offering doesn't deliver absolute value, only that it doesn't deliver more value than the next best alternative.

You can think of the points of parity as table stakes or the cost of doing business. They represent the right to play in your market, like meeting industry standards or having technical literature in the correct language. Customers expect you to deliver that value element or they won't even consider your offering.

That brings us to the one variation on points of parity: the value element customers expect that your offering doesn't currently deliver. This may be true for a new offering or for an existing offering with a select segment of customers. We call this a negative parity element (or P-). It is still not quantified but if you don't address it, you will never be able sell to that customer group.

In general, you are not likely to win if all you do is fix the negatives, but you can certainly lose if you ignore them.

Differentiation (D)

Differentiation (D), a slightly more exciting classification, means that your offering is measurably better (or worse) than the next best alternative in a way that customers will recognize.

There are two types of points of differentiation:

- D+ elements, where your offering delivers more value than the next best alternative

- D- elements, where the next best alternative actually delivers more value than your offering

This is one area where you need to be brutally honest with yourself. If a competitor is better at something, then acknowledge it and quantify what that means for the customer. If you don't find any D- elements, you probably need to dig deeper because it is likely that your competitors are better than you in at least one thing.

Conversely, don't fret if you find some big D- elements. In the end, hopefully your D+ elements are more significant than your competitor's differentiators (D-), at least for your targeted groups of customers, as we will discuss in Chapter 6 (Segmentation).

Opportunity (O)

The last, and the most exciting, classification is Opportunity (O). These elements are only found through a deep understanding of what a customer should want. Opportunities are things that the customer isn't asking for, but would solve a big problem if you could do it.

Examples of such opportunities are Henry Ford and the Model T, iTunes, and Uber. No one asked for any of these things, yet each of them obviously solved a large problem for their customers.

Not every opportunity will be a game-changer, but it can often lead to significant differentiation for a sustained period of time. If you can legitimately be the first to create a unique capability, it can be a game changer, especially if you your business model makes it sustainable.

In theory there might also be an O-, something that no one is doing today that no customer would value. If you are working on projects like that, you might want to redirect your efforts as O-'s will never factor into the value equation.

Right to Win

As we mentioned previously, points of parity are usually the right to play. Differentiators and opportunities form your right to win. The only things that need to be quantified in your value equation are your positive differentiators (D+) plus any opportunities (O) minus your negative differentiators (D-). That usually creates a much shorter and manageable list of value elements to quantify, and a more practical way to use the value equation.

Value in the Value Chain

Let's revisit that fundamental question, "Who is your customer?" A few years ago, most sales training classes would say that your customer is the person that can place an order with you.

For most B2B offerings, however, the answer to who places the order is either a distributor or purchasing agent. But are distributors or purchasing agents in a position to really understand and appreciate the value that you deliver in an end-use application? In other words, are they the most important customers?

The complete answer to the question is that your customer is anyone who receives value, influences the buying decision, is necessary for you to deliver value, or makes the final purchase decision.

As discussed in Chapter 3 (Opportunity and Market Definition), too many companies only look at the next level in the value chain when they look at customer value when in fact, the value they create is actually two, three, or even four steps down the chain.

Here is a great example of this from one of our Grassroots Strategy sessions.

Our client sold a pigment that was used in automotive paints. They developed a new pigment based on technology that significantly improved a car's visual appearance. European car companies, for whom it is standard practice to upcharge for premium paints, charged up to 800 € per vehicle for premium paint that required only about 100 grams (0.10 kg) of pigment per vehicle.

Our client could show that more dramatic paint effects correlated with higher upcharges from the vehicle makers. With a little math, they could estimate that the value created was more than 3,000 € per kg. Their typical selling price for additives was around 250 €.

This was very exciting until the project leader approached us during the session and said, "This is great stuff, but we have already set the price at 280 €." We asked if we had calculated the value incorrectly but the project manager said, "No, it all seems right, but the customer told us that they wouldn't pay more than 300 €. A higher price just doesn't feel right."

Any time the concept of how a price "feels" comes up in B2B pricing discussions, alarms should go off in your head. B2B pricing is not about feeling, it's about value. What "feels right" is almost certainly based on an internal reference point, not an external view of value.

Obviously, this raised a red flag for us. As a rule, customers will never tell you what they are really willing to pay and even if they do, you should be very careful how you interpret their response. So, we asked why they thought the customer wouldn't pay more than 300 €.

Their answer? Because the customer was currently paying 250 €. The customer acknowledged that our client had spent money developing this new technology and they were willing to pay more, but not a lot more. Hence the price of 280 €, which was below the theoretical price limit of 300 €.

We then asked which customer gave them this response. Only then did they admit it was a paint company that is their direct customer. Now it made sense. If you were a paint company and your supplier asked you how much more you would pay for a pigment that is already a significant percentage of your bill of materials, the answer would be as little as possible.

Had the client talked to one of the car companies, they would have gotten a very different answer. As it turned out, there was already a pigment on the market that was priced at 2,000 €, so the cap of 300 € wasn't real. Our client finally launched their pigment at a list price of about 2,700 € per kg and after a year, were maintaining a net price of 2,200 €.

The Value Function

How do customers actually receive value? Is value always a linear function where a 10% increase in the attribute delivering customer value always create a 10% increase in value? The short answer is no. How a customer receives value can come in many forms. Value can be linear to a degree, but there is often a cap after which there is no additional value.

As an example, let's imagine a solution that helps a field service organization shorten the time it takes to deliver the service. If a typical service call is one hour and the travel time to each call is 30 minutes, does saving five minutes on each call save any money?

Not likely, because the service rep can still only handle five calls in an eight-hour day. You would need to save at least 10 minutes per call to raise capacity to six calls per day, so the value is a step function, not linear. Taken to the extreme, if you cut the call time down to five or 10 minutes, the 30-minute drive time limits the ability to do any more calls, so there is also a ceiling on the value of shortening service call time.

Value can be received with linear and step functions, and it can also be all or nothing. Suppose you manufacture engines for corporate jets, and you're trying to build an engine whose range is from New York to Shanghai, one of the longest distances that would be needed by a business traveler. How much value is there in an engine that can get you to within 100 miles of Shanghai? None, really. But, there would be significant value if you could reach Shanghai without needing to stop to refuel.

On the other hand, how much value is there being able to fly 500 miles beyond Shanghai? None, right? The value of not having to stop and refuel in Anchorage is huge, especially in terms of an executive's time. But that value is received as soon as you can reach Shanghai and beyond that doesn't matter. That is an all or nothing proposition.

Value can also take the form of an S-curve, which has areas where little value is derived from improvements in the attribute, and other areas where large amounts of value are derived by small changes in the attribute.

Bottom line, you must really understand your customer's business and how your offering impacts their business to understand the value function.

Value Identification

This seems pretty easy so far, right? Just find ways to deliver value to your customer and you can sell more and hopefully charge more.

However, in order to truly know how to deliver more value, you need an intimate understanding of their business and how they make money. We call that becoming a "student of your customer." The goal is to know your customer's business so well that you can identify problems and ways to improve performance before they even know there's an issue.

Your customers probably spend far more time trying to understand your cost structure in an effort to get you to reduce your price than you spend trying to understand value in order to charge a higher price. Anyone who has ever been subjected to a "should cost" model knows that to be true.

Customers sometimes reverse-engineer your product to estimate the materials, labor, and other conversion costs that go into making it. Then they build a "should cost" model that provides what they think is a "fair" margin over your estimated cost. We can guarantee that what they believe is fair is much less than your owners and investors expect as a return on their investment. It is your job to understand value and show them how they "should value" your offering because of the economic performance it will provide to their business.

One of the best ways to identify value is to systematically observe their business. Watch them operate, ask why they do certain things, and find areas where they could improve.

There is an age-old story about a metals company that required all of its sales reps to spend one day per month touring a customer facility, and on that day they were forbidden from selling or taking an order. Their only job was to follow their product through the customer's plant and document what they observed.

On one such visit, a sales rep watched as a shipment of their metal rod was unloaded from a truck. As soon as the pallet was unloaded from the truck, the foreman left to make a call. When the rep asked why, he learned that the 24-foot length of rod was too long to make the turn to enter the warehouse. They needed a mechanic to cut the rod in half and stack it on two pallets. The rep asked if it would be better if they shipped their rods in 12-foot lengths to which the customer replied, "That would be fantastic, but you don't have 12-foot lengths in your catalogue."

How much value would it create to fix that issue? Since the metal rod is a commodity, the relative value created was huge. Are you able to price to that value? Probably not in this case, since shipping in 12-foot lengths is easily copied. But you just created enough value to keep this customer loyal, even if you aren't always the cheapest option. And if some corporate purchasing manager decides to switch suppliers and go back to 24-foot lengths, do you think

they'll get an angry call from this loading dock supervisor?
Absolutely.

Beyond systematic observation, another way to understand value is
to partner with one or two key customers for joint product
development. You can also provide your offering free of charge to
select customers in exchange for information and metrics about the
impact it had on their business.

The worst way to determine how much a customer is willing to pay
for your offering is to ask directly. As we said earlier, the answer will
always be less for more. When you aren't able to get to an
understanding of value, where should you start on your price? The
answer is always embarrassingly high. Customers will let you know
if you are overpriced by not buying, but if you are underpriced
relative to the value you create, the market may quietly say thank
you, but you will never know.

Value Leakage

When it comes to value, there are four ways that companies don't
capture the value that they create. Three are bad, but one is
necessary.

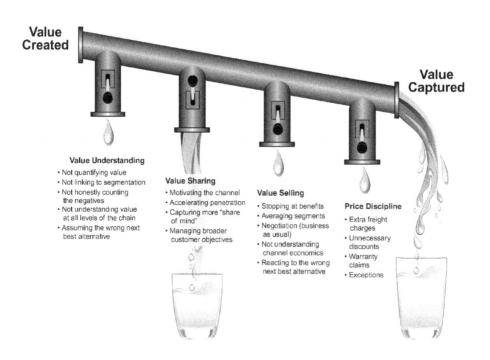

Value Created

Value Captured

Value Understanding
- Not quantifying value
- Not linking to segmentation
- Not honestly counting the negatives
- Not understanding value at all levels of the chain
- Assuming the wrong next best alternative

Value Sharing
- Motivating the channel
- Accelerating penetration
- Capturing more "share of mind"
- Managing broader customer objectives

Value Selling
- Stopping at benefits
- Averaging segments
- Negotiation (business as usual)
- Not understanding channel economics
- Reacting to the wrong next best alternative

Price Discipline
- Extra freight charges
- Unnecessary discounts
- Warranty claims
- Exceptions

Let's start with the one that's necessary: value sharing. In order to get your customer, and all entities within the channel, to change what they're doing and buy your offering, you must share value with them.

If you create $100 of value, you will not be able to capture all of that value. You need to share some of it with channel partners and especially with the end customer, or else they have no economic incentive to buy from you.

Now on to the value leakage forces you should avoid. The most common, and most fatal, is simply not understanding value in the first place. If you don't know how much your offering improves your customer's business, how can you price to that value?

Next is value capture, which starts with not pricing to value. Even if you understand value, if you don't price your offering to capture an appropriate part of that value, you are losing the battle. We talk more about this in Chapter 8 (Value Pricing) but for now, your price should always be based on the value you create and not your cost. Your salesforce needs to understand how to use this in negotiations or you risk giving it all away.

There are other ways you can fail to capture value. One of the biggest is reacting to the wrong next best alternative. If a customer tells you that they like your offering but you are priced 30% above your competitor, you shouldn't jump immediately to offer a discount. Is the customer really comparing apples to apples? Are you creating enough value to justify the 30% price premium over your competitor?

This is the example we discussed earlier in this chapter under Trap 5 (Focusing on the Wrong Next Best Alternative). It's the one where the customer tells the Mercedes dealership that they really want one of its cars, but then shows a Hyundai ad and says this is the price they want to pay. The dealership would likely tell them to hit the road and go talk to Hyundai. Why would you accept the same behavior from your customers?

Systematic price leakage is the last value leakage mechanism. Most transactional pricing initiatives are designed to target these issues. A transactional pricing initiative looks at things like terms and conditions, volume discounts given even when the customer didn't hit their volume commitments, stacked discounts, and warranty claims.

When companies look for these leakages, they typically discover potential price improvements of two to three percent. These improvements can be significant since price increases drop straight to the bottom line; however, value understanding and value capture can often identify potential changes with more value and significantly more impact.

Bottom line, you must share value with customers and the channel, but watch out for unnecessary value leakage. Make sure you understand value, make sure you price and defend that value to capture it, and periodically evaluate your actual pricing to reduce price leakage.

Sustaining Value

Now that you have identified customer value, quantified it, priced and sold based on that value, and avoided price leakage, get ready because the work has only begun. Now you have to defend that value over time.

What happens to all prices and differentiation over time? Competitors catch up and the prices will go down. Said differently, points of opportunity become points of differentiation and eventually points of parity, as competitors get better at copying your offering. So ideally, you want to be sure that you can sustain the value that you create.

As we will discuss in more detail in Chapter 8 (Value Pricing), your ability to maintain differentiation over time is key to your ability to capture value, no matter how much value you create initially.

Think about the sources of your value advantage on a continuum from the least sustainable (we merely assemble parts available to anyone, like a PC box manufacturer in the 1990s) to the most sustainable (we have a patent that precludes anyone else from doing what we do).

Here are some key questions that you need to honestly answer.

- How easy is it to copy what you're doing?

- How long will it take a competitor to copy it?

- Can the customer find another way to solve the problem that you solve?

- Can you protect your differentiation with a patent or with trade secrets?

- Can you deliver value with a different business model where you continually get better at a rate such that the competition can never catch up?

You have probably gathered that we are big fans of these types of flywheel businesses. It's always exciting to create something that gets better every time you do it, where you gain more knowledge and experience, and where you build scale that makes it difficult for others to compete. We will talk more about building a flywheel business in Chapter 9 (Business Model).

In the end, you need to understand how your differentiation creates value for your customer, and how sustainable that differentiation really is.

Summary

We believe differentiation that creates economic value for a customer is the basis for a good strategy. The most successful B2B companies are those that continually find ways to leverage differentiation, either existing or new, to create economic value by solving problems in their customers' businesses. Often those same customers don't even realize they have a problem.

One of our favorite quotes about asking customers what they need is attributed to Henry Ford: "If I had asked people what they wanted, they would have said faster horses." Regardless of whether Ford actually uttered those words, the sentiment is still true.

Customers can't articulate a need for a solution they don't know exists. If asked differently, Ford may have uncovered that customers really needed a faster way to get from point A to point B, but no one at the time could have asked for a mass-produced automobile. It's your job to figure out what they should want, based on their desired outcomes and business model, combined with what you know is possible.

Before we move on to segmentation, remember that value is always:

- Customer specific

- Measured in currency

- Relative to the next best alternative

Value is not always easy to understand, which is why it can be so rewarding to adopt the concept of customer value across your organization.

Value is customer specific, so presumably we would do well to have different offerings, service levels and/or prices by customer. Since it is not always possible to tailor all these to the individual customer, it is often helpful to group customers who value similar things. We call that process segmentation, and it is the topic of the next chapter.

6

Segmentation

One-size-fits-all may be great for operational efficiency, but it rarely works for marketing and selling to customers. Most customers want the size that actually fits them, not something that works "on average." In 1909, when Henry Ford was building cars for the multitudes, he said that customers could have a car in any color "so long as it is black." This helped Ford mass produce cars at a low cost, but it only worked as a strategy until the competition began to offer color choices. Your customers are no different. One size does not fit all!

One of our clients calls this the "medium-sized T-shirt problem." You can do a detailed study of the market and conclude that the average customer needs a medium-sized T-shirt. But in reality, people don't buy T-shirts for the average customer, they buy them for themselves. As soon as another vendor offers sizes to fit each group of customers, your potential customer base shrinks to the fraction of customers who really need a medium. You have some chance with customers who need a small, since they can wear a medium if nothing else is available, but virtually no chance with customers who need an extra-large.

Although this may sound obvious, you'd be surprised how often we see B2B companies that, schooled in Six Sigma and focused on efficiency by driving out variation, design for the average/highest volume/favorite customer without considering that different customers may need different things.

Going to market without segmenting is like going outside without checking the weather. You can dress for the average day and occasionally be right, or you can walk out in Cleveland in April to a snowstorm. With a little research, you can be prepared for what you might expect.

Why Should You Segment Your Market?

In our Grassroots Strategy sessions, we often joke about whether customer value or market segmentation is more important. The truth is that they go hand-in-hand, and neither is of much use without the other.

Still, we sometimes refer to segmentation as the heart of strategic marketing, and for good reason. As Dr. Nas Narayandas of Harvard University said, "In business-to-business, the customers you select are the company you will become."

Since value is customer specific, the goal of segmentation is finding groups of customers that value similar things. If you get this right, you can tailor your offerings and prices to more precisely meet the needs of your customers. You might even do a better job identifying the customers you should avoid and screening them out early before spending resources on an opportunity that is unlikely to ever become profitable.

Valid market segmentation is critical to building a profitable growth engine. It can help maximize your return on investment in R&D and manufacturing, build more effective offerings for your target customers, provide a focus for sales to target deals, and close more of them.

To understand why segmentation is important, look no further than your income statement. Segmentation, or failure to segment, is central to the success of your business because it impacts both the revenue and the cost side of your P&L. It's not just a PowerPoint exercise for the marketing department. Segmentation, done well, is actually an enabler for a more profitable business.

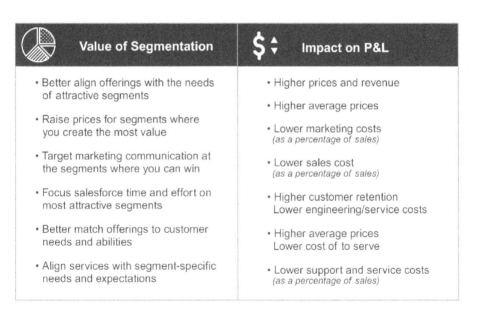

Value of Segmentation	Impact on P&L
• Better align offerings with the needs of attractive segments	• Higher prices and revenue
• Raise prices for segments where you create the most value	• Higher average prices
	• Lower marketing costs *(as a percentage of sales)*
• Target marketing communication at the segments where you can win	• Lower sales cost *(as a percentage of sales)*
• Focus salesforce time and effort on most attractive segments	• Higher customer retention Lower engineering/service costs
• Better match offerings to customer needs and abilities	• Higher average prices Lower cost of to serve
• Align services with segment-specific needs and expectations	• Lower support and service costs *(as a percentage of sales)*

What Is Segmentation?

We must give credit for our definition of a segment to our long-time colleague and mentor, Professor Emeritus Dr. Stewart W. Bither of the The Smeal College of Business Administration at Penn State University.

As a basic definition, segments are groups of customers that share similar need hierarchies; that is, they want and will pay for similar things. So, while you may currently use the word segment to describe a business segment or an end-use market, it is only really a segment if the customers in that group need the same thing. Anything else is just a customer or product classification, not a segmentation scheme.

Sounds simple, right? A segment is a segment if all customers need the same thing or react similarly to the same value proposition, as we'll see in the next chapter. But like many things in life, this definition is deceptively simple.

For starters, it's important to understand that although segments may exist in a theoretical sense, they need to be discovered. In other words, they are not useful until they are conceptualized. Not everyone looking at the same group of customers will segment them the same way. As we tell our clients, your aim should be to develop and deploy a segmentation scheme that aligns with your differentiated capabilities. This may not be the same scheme that works best for your competitors.

Most companies will benefit from the transformative power of successful segmentation. As one of our long-time customers explains: "*We are looking for groups of customers that really need what we do well, and whose next best alternative is both ugly and expensive.*" That is the essence of segmentation: a more complete articulation of your sweet spots as described in Chapter 1 (What is Strategy?).

It's also important to remember that we have a very specific definition of "need." As we learned in Chapter 4 (Microeconomics), a need is a want combined with a willingness to pay. It is not about customer preference or attitudinal surveys. Rather, you must dig into your customer's economics and understand what they should be willing to pay more for.

To appreciate the benefits of effectively segmenting your market, consider the dangers of not doing it or not doing it correctly. If your competitors successfully segment the market and you don't, over time you will be left with only the customers that no one else wants. This is rarely a route to improving profitability.

The (Soon to Be Famous) Dog Food Story

Let's dive into segmentation with an iconic example from the consumer realm: segmentation of the dog food market.

Until at least the mid-1980s, dog food manufacturers and marketers segmented their market along two dimensions: the age and size of the dog. Dogs were either puppies, adults, or old and they were either big or small.

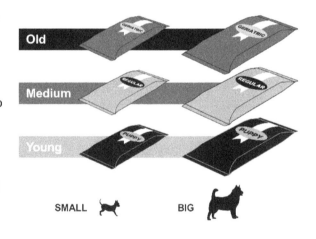

Recognizing the different needs of "senior" dogs was seen as a major breakthrough with the introduction of Cycle brand dog food, which included "a lower calorie blend for older, less active dogs." Apparently, diet food for fat dogs didn't get past the copy editors, although that's what this was.

Note: Like any good legend, this story has been told and retold many times with little formal documentation. We have been unable to confirm the details with primary sources and are forced to conclude that some of the story may be apocryphal. However, it is memorable, and more importantly contains some great lessons.

Dog food companies also considered another dimension: product form. Is it wet food, dry food, or a treat? You can think of this as a third dimension that intersects with age and size. This aspect is tangential to our story and besides, it makes the illustration harder to draw.

The thinking was that each group of dogs had different needs; therefore, each group needed its own product. And not surprisingly, dog food companies came up with products aimed at these different groupings. If your dog was small, you bought dog food that was chopped into bite-sized pieces and sold in smaller containers. If your dog was old, you bought dog food that had fewer calories and more of the nutrients that older dogs need.

But is this a meaningful segmentation when the goal of segmentation is to improve profitability? For starters, it's hard to differentiate when the whole industry segments the same way. The goal is to segment based on the needs you can address best, or the needs no one else is addressing and that you can address first. Your goal should be to find "a group of customers who really need what you do well and for whom their next best alternative is ugly and expensive."

This product-based market view isn't great, but it does offer some advantages. One is that all dog food companies reported their data in the same categories. As a result, they knew their market share by "segment" to a tenth of a percentage point. Junior brand managers could have a field day writing memos explaining why they gained two-tenths of a share point in small dog puppy food.

The other advantage of product-based segmentation is that each segment corresponds to a specific product or small subset of products. This is important because most companies are product-centric and are typically organized around product managers.

And, products are tangible. For example, you need to plan and schedule production at the product level. How much of each item should be manufactured? How much of each size should be stocked in each warehouse? These are very real operating decisions, and this type of segmentation links directly to those decisions.

By now you probably suspect that this segmentation is incomplete and doesn't fully reflect our definition of "needs-based segmentation." It is based on needs but in an almost trivial way because it reflects differences in the nutritional needs among dogs of different ages and sizes.

But therein lies the biggest problem: it is a segmentation of dogs. And while dogs are the ultimate consumers of dog food and may even accompany their owners to the pet store, dogs are not the primary decision maker. We've all heard rumors of dogs receiving credit card offers in the mail, but we're pretty sure it's the dog's owner who pays for its food at the checkout counter.

Let's go a step further. What if we were to segment dog owners based on their personal needs? Do you think canine nutrition would be their foremost decision factor? Observation makes it clear that different people have different types of dogs for different reasons. As a result, their willingness to pay to make their dog happy may also be vastly different. Compare the farm dog that sleeps outside to the pampered little purse dog who accompanies her owner on the red carpet. Which owner is more likely to pay more to feed their dog?

A Little History

It's worth reviewing the backstory that led to this sweeping change in the dog food industry. By the mid-1980s, most major brands were owned by the emerging consumer packaged goods conglomerates. These companies were well-versed in market research techniques and they applied them to the dog food market as they had in other categories.

One technique uses "household panel data" that tracks household consumption over time and across multiple channels and occasions. As such, it is very useful for tracking trends that cannot be picked up using retail point of sale data alone, like the rise of consumer warehouse clubs or the resurgence of farmer's markets.

While digging through household panel data going back to the mid-1950s, one company discovered that 15% to 20% of households with a dog did not report buying any dog-specific food. This makes sense in a historical context. In the 1950s, families had less discretionary income and more families lived on farms where dogs could fend for themselves. Big family meals with enough leftovers for the dog were the norm.

However, this 15% to 20% stayed relatively constant through the early 1980s. This hardly made sense given the near revolution in how Americans ate during this time period. First, there was a massive shift in food spending to "away from home" consumption, particularly fast food where there were rarely any leftovers. There was the proliferation of the microwave oven and single-serve meals. Additionally, families were getting smaller, moving into urban areas, and had more discretionary income to spend on their pets. So why weren't more families buying dog food?

The surprising answer was uncovered by holding customer focus groups with these customers. Instead of feeding leftovers to their dogs, many of them were intentionally preparing an extra portion of "people food" and feeding it to the dog!

After conducting additional research with dog owners, the company came up with a new segmentation based on how dog owners think about their dogs.

Each segment was accompanied by a demographic description of the typical dog owner in that segment and the needs that differentiate them from other types of owners.

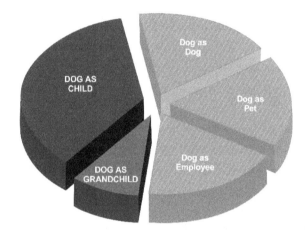

As you can see, "Dog as Child" is the largest segment and as the name implies, these owners had a fairly high willingness to pay. But although the "Dog as Grandchild" segment is smaller, these owners had an even higher willingness to pay. This is where you find people preparing an extra helping of Salisbury steak and putting it on a plate for their dogs.

The biggest problem with the old segmentation now becomes clear. Because they segmented products and not customers, their segmentation didn't even include customers buying and cooking people food for their dogs. In other words, those customers who displayed the highest willingness to pay.

It is worth repeating that the customers who were willing to spend the most to feed their dogs were nowhere in the old segmentation. Hence there was no way to find them, much less inquire about their needs and target them with products and messaging.

We will talk about value proposition in Chapter 7 but for now, can you envision the winning offering for these segments with a high willingness to pay? When asked why they invested so much time and expense in preparing meals for their dog, these owners were almost unanimous in their response: "Well, look how much she loves it!" And there it is. They were fulfilling their need to spoil their dog, even if at some level they knew that "people food" is not the healthiest long-term food option for dogs.

So, the winning value proposition would be something like this: "Your dog will love our dog food as much as people food, but it's healthier for them." And it turns out that while you can price this product at a premium because the next best alternative is expensive and time-consuming, you don't have to add too much cost. You simply make the dog food out of what dogs are meant to eat (we'll leave out the details of dog food ingredients, in case you're eating) and add a few drops of gravy or other aromatic ingredient so it looks and smells like something the owner would eat after opening the package.

If you were a competitor at the time, chances are you would never have seen this coming. Nor would you have even seen it happening at first, because you'd still be thinking about the market in the same old way. What you would have seen is a company launching a product for a target you could not understand, as it cuts across your "segments." And when it did start to sell, you might not have seen it as a loss in market share because initially, the new product would have taken sales primarily from the butcher counter, not other dog food brands.

This kind of new thinking allowed a company to start selling premium dog food and building a position in the market no one had recognized before. When competitors eventually do react, they will be behind in terms of both their product line and their understanding of this segment.

Although new segments are difficult to quantify (the product isn't labeled "dog food for people who think of their dogs as grandchildren") and there is no industry report that tells you the exact size of this segment, their strategic value is that they represent new ways of targeting high-value customers.

But enough history. Let's fast forward to today. No doubt these segments have evolved. For example, since the US population has aged, the "Dog as Grandchild" segment has almost certainly grown. In addition, the new "Dog as Fashion Accessory" segment may be willing to spend even more money to spoil their dogs.

We have also seen an explosion in spending on dog-related products that goes well beyond dog food. By one account, the dog food industry represented more than $60 billion in revenue in 2015, up from well less than $1 billion in the early 1980s (Bureau). And today, you can buy organic and gluten-free dog food, and even food that is custom-designed based on a sample of your dog's DNA.

Marketers tend to think of segmentation schemes that are easy to quantify, link to existing products, and can be consistently reported over time. Many would have looked at the old segmentation scheme as "the way we've always done it" and never raised any questions.

But it's always better and more powerful to segment the market based on the needs of the customer. And sometimes, segmenting on needs that reflect points of difference can lead to intriguing ways to increase value. That's why segmentation is inherently a creative process: there is no "paint by numbers" path that will lead you to ideas you haven't thought of yet.

Although dog food is a consumer product, there are some important lessons from the dog food story that apply to the B2B world as well.

- Segment the right customer or the right level of customer, which is why you start with the value chain.

- Product classification is NOT segmentation, although it may be necessary to run the business.

- Needs-based segments can be difficult to quantify precisely and require ongoing investment to stay fresh.

- To be actionable, needs-based segments must be associated with clearly defined customer characteristics or demographics. For example, empty-nesters with discretionary income and real grandchildren living far away probably fall into the "Dog as Grandchild" segment. In a B2B context, this may be something like "customers in highly-regulated, high-energy cost markets."

- Segmenting in different ways can unlock previously unseen opportunities, sources of value and possibly unseen customers, to create and capture additional profit opportunities.

A Tale of Two Earbuds

In another consumer example, we see how engineers narrowly defined the earbud market based on technology instead of customer needs. As the market began maturing in the 1990s, companies defined market segments in terms of a single dimension of product performance. Earbuds were considered low, medium, or high-end based entirely on sound quality; specifically, their ability to replicate the "etymotic curve," or the human ear's range of frequencies. Not surprisingly, prices also correlated with this single dimension resulting in a "good-better-best" marketing approach.

This made a lot of sense to the audio engineers designing products for the market. Since they were mostly audiophiles themselves and spent a lot of time thinking about the etymotic curve, clearly they knew what was "best" for everyone else.

In 2003, Skullcandy was the first earbud company to realize that consumers might care about more than purely audio quality (Alden & Tiku, 2008). They started with the insight that young people, and especially young men, cared more about the amount of bass.

The first product they launched was "Skull Crusher" earbuds with amped-up bass (Kremkau, 2007). Besides being a rousing success, it turned out that making speakers with amped-up bass leveraged low-end speaker technology and was cheaper than producing those with better sound quality. In fact, they were cheaper to make than even the "good" earbuds but that doesn't mean they were priced that way!

Skullcandy also realized that its target customer wasn't shopping in high-end consumer electronics stores. Rather, they frequented places like snowboard and skate shops. Thus, they were able to focus their marketing efforts in those channels rather than focusing on traditional music channels.

Over time, Skullcandy started getting into fashion elements and endorsements. They weren't necessarily making a "better" product by traditional metrics. They just figured out how to meet a need that aligned with what a segment of the market wanted. As a result, they are now the third largest provider of earbuds in the US.

Established players in this market took too long to respond to Skullcandy's new way of thinking. By the time a competitor has recognized a need and developed a product and system for serving that need, it's often too late and very difficult for them to catch up. The evidence for this is that even though other players now make "amped-up bass" earbuds, they sell very few.

Bose had previously pursued a similar strategy when it realized that people sometimes listen to music primarily to avoid ambient sound. So, they built an entire business around headphones designed to cancel out noise. They commercialized the technology to support the idea, and then developed the messaging to get their product to this market segment. Most major manufacturers now make noise-cancelling headphones, but Bose still dominates this market segment.

It's worth repeating that segmentation, done well, can keep you at the top of your market for decades. While ear buds and dog food are B2C examples, they hold two key lessons that are perhaps even more common in the B2B world:

1. You need to understand what "better" means to each group of customers, because relying on your engineers to design what they think is best is rarely a good idea.

2. If you can establish a leading position with a given segment (especially if you are the first to discover that segment), you can refine your offering and your targeting over time in ways that are difficult to copy, often allowing you to maintain or expand your market share.

Segmenting Markets by Needs

A market segment is not actually a segment unless you can define needs that are fundamentally different from other segments. The key is to identify needs from the customer perspective instead of looking only at product features. Generally speaking, there are three types of needs you should investigate.

- **Functional.** A functional need is typically all or nothing in that a customer either needs it or they don't. If you're a scuba diver and need to take pictures, you need a waterproof camera that works underwater. If you're not a scuba diver, then a camera being waterproof probably doesn't factor into your buying decision.

  Regulations may drive functional needs for B2B organizations. Tractors sold in the US or Europe must meet the highest emission standards, but that's not the case if they're being sold in India, where emissions standards can be one or two generations behind.

- **Economic.** In this case, the offering impacts different customer economics in different ways and the value is relative as opposed to either/or. For example, everyone values lower utility costs. However, the need to save electricity is much greater for a customer running off a diesel generator that's nearing capacity than it is for a customer buying inexpensive hydroelectric power for three cents per kilowatt hour.

  A need is a willingness to spend, so a customer will spend more (or trade off something else) to save electricity if their electric rate or utility costs are higher.

- **Emotional.** Consumer markets primarily segment by emotional needs, as demonstrated in the dog food story. Emotional needs are generally less relevant in B2B where a procurement department is often involved and purchasing managers have been trained to remove emotion from decision making. But ignoring emotional needs entirely can also lead you astray.

  Within limits, customers sometimes need to feel affiliation or association with a respectable company. Or they may need to feel confident that they are buying from someone who will support them down the road. This is especially true when the buyer is not an expert and the project is hard to fully define, such as consulting engagements or big software installations.

In the B2C world, segmentation is often geared toward the functional and/or emotional needs of customers. Let's compare how that plays out in two newspapers: *The New York Times* and *USA Today*.

Until the mid-1980s, *The New York Times* was the leading newspaper in the country with the highest market share. But when *USA Today* launched in 1982 with broad distribution and brightly-colored graphics, it quickly gained ground (USAToday, n.d.). *USA Today* looked and read nothing like *The New York Times* but it grew in volume as a national paper in part because it was often given away for free at hotels.

How should *The New York Times* have responded to this challenge? Instinctively you might say the answer was to start looking and sounding more like *USA Today*. They might have chosen to add color, cut back on dense articles and heavy reporting, reduce the reading level to fourth grade, and offer more light news on entertainment. This is what we call a "me too" mentality and is not a proper response. It is usually unwise to mimic your competitor. Like your mother probably said more than once, "everyone else is doing it" is not a good enough reason.

If you feel some urgency to respond, start by looking at market needs. Instead of going after the *USA Today* market segment on a national level, *The New York Times* fashioned itself as a New York-based newspaper serving a national audience. They realized that many people outside New York City valued in-depth news analysis and could read at a twelfth-grade level, so they created regional versions for other metro areas and dramatically expanded distribution outside New York City.

This is a great example of a functional segmentation. *USA Today* and *The New York Times* are newspapers that serve different functions and therefore, different market segments. You read *USA Today* for a quick update on sports and headlines as you eat breakfast in your hotel. You read *The New York Times* for detailed coverage of more complicated issues or to catch up on arts and literature over a leisurely cup of coffee on a Sunday morning.

This is a case where the same customer may actually be in two different segments at different times when they have different needs. Even today, New York City commuters may read one paper for business news on the train into work and another with more light entertainment on the train ride home – different offerings serving different functions.

How to Segment a B2B Market

Business-to-business marketing is all about value. You grow your business by identifying customers that should want a certain product or solution based on the economics of their business.

The best segmentations identify groups of customers making similar trade-offs, reflecting a similar willingness to pay for similar offerings. They also reflect an understanding of the factors that distinguish these customers from other segments. They push beyond buyer behavior to articulate fundamental differences between companies, not the different personalities of the purchasing managers. This is an important distinction from consumer segmentations, which often start with customer personas.

While this can be complex, there is generally little value in over-simplified segmentations. Neither is complex always better. We have seen countless examples of customer segmentations that were statistically valid, but had no practical way to predict which segment a potential customer was in. As such, these segmentation schemes were completely worthless for determining what to offer to which customer and how to price it. To state the obvious, if you can only tell what segment a customer is in after they make a purchase, that's self-selection, not segmentation.

B2B marketers sometimes try to copy consumer marketers by segmenting based solely on customer demographics and/or psychographics. This usually works in consumer marketing because is often primarily concerned with messaging. Everyone sees the same box of cereal on the shelf, but some may be influenced to believe its claimed health benefits will transform their life.

The key to effective B2B segmentation is to find patterns in customer characteristics that match differences in underlying needs. For a segmentation scheme to be valuable, it must be based on how your offering delivers value to its customers relative to other alternatives. In other words, why do some customers need some elements more than others? And then what characteristics do those customers tend to share? Without a clear link to differences in customer needs, you will never have a usable B2B segmentation.

For example, two customers may run the same manufacturing process, but one who can only access polluted water for use in their process likely has very different filtration needs than one with access to inexpensive clean water. The different customer characteristics predict a qualitatively different need.

Proper segmentation incorporates the following:

- Defines what you are segmenting and the size of the market universe

- Identifies who or what dictates the value you deliver (end-customer or distributor, application, buying occasion, etc.)

- Understands the key problems faced by your customers

- Understands and articulates your potential differentiation

- Finds the needs that discriminate among customers: why do some customers need more of what you offer than others?

- Links these discriminating needs to customer characteristics in order to identify target segments in advance

- Develops unique value propositions for each target segment (more on this in Chapter 7 (Value Propositions))

- Links segmentation to the business model and ultimately your go-to-market plan by changing how you serve different segments (offering, price, services, etc.) and providing explicit guidelines on how the sales force should treat different customers based on their segment

Segments are relevant and strategically actionable only if they relate to what you do differently than your competitors. That's why we caution our clients against using segments from industry reports.

Because these segments are available to your competitors as well, they are an inadequate way to segment your customers and do not provide you with any advantage.

Worse, they can actually be misleading, causing you to target a segment that everyone else is chasing as opposed to finding the segment that really needs what you do well.

Sample Segmentation: Truck Parts

Suppose you sell parts that are used to repair and upgrade mechanical systems on trucks in China. Much of the market buys cheap local stuff. However, your parts deliver better performance and break down less frequently, allowing customers to go long distances with more certainty of arriving on time.

Because your goal is to find a market that will pay for your parts, you purchase a report that provides a segmentation of the market.

There you find four segments:

- Older drivers
- Mini-fleets
- New drivers
- Struggling drivers

Forty-one percent of the market is older drivers that typically have one truck and buy parts from suppliers they already know. Mini-fleets have multiple trucks and need quicker turnaround on service. New drivers tend to be younger and drive longer routes. Strugglers are those not making a lot of money.

SITUATION

- We sell parts to repair and upgrade mechanical systems on trucks (e.g., transmissions)

- Much of the market buys cheap, locally made products

- Our differentiation is improved durability and better performance

- We want to find a market segment that will pay for genuine parts and then build an appropriate go-to-market strategy

Segment	Characteristics	Buying Behaviors
Old School • 41% of trucks	• One truck • Older drivers • Stable routes	• Buy from known suppliers • Prefer Chinese Brands
Mini-fleets • 22%	• 2-5 trucks • Mostly middle aged • Flexible routes	• Prefer commonality across fleet • Want quick-turnaround on service
Newcomers • 25%	• One truck, generally their first • Younger drivers • Longer routes	• Limited loyalty to brands or channels • Willingness to pay for comfort and convenience
Strugglers • 25%	• One truck • Can be any age • Trucks idle nearly • 50 percent of the time	• Limited ability to pay for upgrades • Mostly do-it-yourself maintenance

How do you figure out which segment to target? Our core message has been to look for where you offer value that's different than your competitors.

It turns out that the segmentation in this report isn't actually all that useful. It's obvious you shouldn't put much effort into selling to strugglers and you probably want to avoid older drivers who prefer Chinese parts. That leaves a chunk of the market with no clear indication for a strategy. And you're still a long way from segmentation that defines a winning position in the market.

A better way to think about segments might be based on the cost of failure to the driver – an economic need. This need is most directly influenced by what the driver is transporting and the length of their route.

If they're driving with a load of fresh produce, then they're concerned about perishability and timing, unlike drivers transporting timber. Thinking about the market in this way reveals obvious targets that are naturally willing to pay more to avoid downtime.

Drivers with longer routes, who are more likely to be far from a repair shop and spare parts should they break down, would place more economic value on the durability of their parts. To restate the obvious, the same is true for drivers hauling valuable and/or perishable loads, some of which may be worth far more than a truckload of fruit. Each hour of downtime prevented is significant in terms of potential loss from theft or damage.

A segmentation combining these two factors would look something like:

A Better Way: Segment by Type of Load

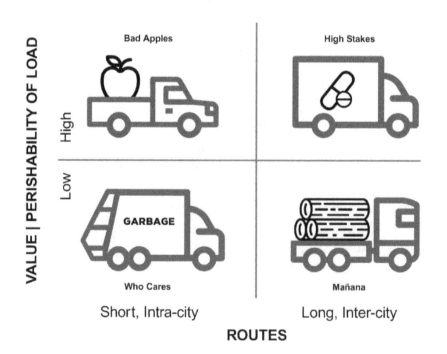

Further, by targeting drivers by distance and type of load, you may have an opportunity to change your business model and reshape the market.

For example, you could go to global pharmaceutical companies whose shipments meet the criteria for the upper right quadrant and put together a "certified driver" program in which the trucking customer pays for the reassurance (risk reduction) that their drivers only use certified parts.

The bottom line is that segmentation done by others is not necessarily useful for your business. In fact, it could even lead you astray or cause you to miss big opportunities.

Focusing on the implications of segmentation changes the way you do things. Always keep in mind that the goal of segmentation is to produce better business results, not just to update charts that stay within the marketing department. Said differently, if you are not willing to intentionally adjust prices, offerings, and sales tactics by customer, then you are probably wasting your time with a segmentation exercise.

The following table shows how you might vary targeting and tactics by segment:

Segment Name	"WHO CARES"	"BAD APPLES"	"MAÑANA"	"HIGH STAKES"
Description	Local transport of low-value loads	Local transport of high-value or perishable loads	Long-haul transport of low-value loads	Long-haul transport of high-value or perishable loads
Example	Garbage Trucks	Local Produce Delivery	Timber Trucks	Pharmaceutical Delivery
Needs	• Lowest Price	• Local Minimize Product Losses	• Minimize Lost Time	• Minimize Product Losses • Minimize Lost Time

Implication	• Ignore this segment	• Secondary Target
		
		• Value Prop = Product Loss
			• Secondary Target
			
			• Value Prop = Productivity
				• Primary Target Value Prop =
				    +Product Loss
				    +Productivity
				
				• Possible Driver Certification

CLEAR TARGET!

Before, all customers received the same brochure, with the same sales coverage, and the same price list with a few volume discounts. Now, sales reps shouldn't call on the Who Cares segment at all, and they would need three very different messages for customers in each of the other segments. Finally, in the High Stakes segment, where the company hiring the truck to ship its goods directly realizes the value, they may be able to create a new business model where this end customer becomes their customer.

Something else you can take from this example is the table. Using this type of table is a convenient way to organize and present your segmentation. More importantly, it is a test of your segmentation. For your segmentation to be real and useful, you have to be able to identify customers with distinct demographics and different needs, and you must be willing to treat them differently (implications).

If you are writing the same things in each column, you do not yet have a useful segmentation.

The table also has long term value in that it can grow as you integrate segmentation into running your business. You could easily add rows to include segment size and growth rates, highlight relevant competitors (next best alternatives), document market share, and compare prices and profitability by segment. It can become an ongoing dashboard to keep segmentation alive as a key to running your business.

What Are You Segmenting?

Clients often wrestle with how granular to make their segmentations. They quickly realize that segmenting at too high a level is meaningless (people who own dogs vs. those who don't), but if they segment at too fine a level it can be too complicated and is often not actionable.

Segmentation is not done in isolation. It must consider the business decision of which markets you want to be in and the tactical decision of allocating sales resources on a daily basis.

One way to think about this is to view your market as a funnel. At the top of the funnel is the addressable market, defined as anyone who could potentially be a customer. While this is important to understand, it is not segmentation because it doesn't distinguish between attractive and unattractive customers.

The second level, target markets, is where segmentation works. It identifies all those customers that might buy from you, how they are different from each other, and how you need to treat them differently.

At the bottom of the funnel is sales targeting, which is where you set priorities within each target segment. For example, you might choose different tactics for current customers and those in countries where you have a better organization in place. They may be in the same segment as other customers, but you can still set priorities based on your ability to serve, the cost to deliver, or the likelihood of winning quickly.

A simple example illustrates how these three levels interact.

If you sell asphalt roofing shingles, your addressable market would be buildings with compatible roof types because no amount of effort would convince someone to put your product over a flat roof or a Spanish tile roof. But that is not yet a segmentation, as it would essentially put every potential customer in a single segment (people who might buy shingles one day).

So, you might segment on dimensions such as the age of the building, the complexity of the roof, the price or value of the structure, whether it's single or multifamily, etc. Remember that these demographic variables are only good segmentation variables if they correlate to differences in underlying needs like warranty period, difficulty of installation or type of support required.

The last consideration would be sales targeting. A good sales trigger is whether there was a recent hailstorm in a particular area. Hailstorms cause roof damage and if the damage is bad enough, insurance companies will pay to replace the roof. So, "receive a free roof inspection and maybe get a new roof and just pay the deductible" becomes a pretty good value proposition.

Although this is a great sales targeting idea that's used in many parts of the country, it is not stable enough to be considered segmentation. You cannot predict in advance which customers will have hail damage next year. Done right, you could still use storms to set short-term sales priorities, and sell different packages depending on the segment you believe each customer to be in. Said differently, segments should be somewhat stable over a multi-year period, not changed week-to-week.

Are Vertical Markets Segments?

We are often asked whether vertical markets are segments. Vertical markets are easily identifiable, such as end-use industries. For example, if you manufacture large industrial motors, you might sell them to paper mills, steel mills and utilities. These are certainly different types of customers with different needs, and each has different knowledge requirements for the person selling to them.

It doesn't take a lot of research to figure out whether a facility makes paper or steel, since it's usually in the name of the company. But be careful before you assume that these are segments.

Make no mistake, if you really understand end-use markets and use this knowledge to guide product development and marketing and sales communications, this is substantially better than treating all customers the same way. However, your competitors can easily do the same thing, so you are significantly better off with a real segmentation based on needs. Some needs may cut across vertical markets and some verticals that have similar needs can be combined into a single segment. If a given vertical is big and important, you may also want to segment within that vertical.

Suppose you sell commercial vinyl flooring to hospitals and schools, among other customers. Those are vertical markets, but are they segments? The answer rests on a difference in needs.

In this case, they are probably in the same segment because they both have large spaces that need relatively inexpensive flooring that is durable and easy to clean. You might segment on some other dimension like the size or age of the building or the ability to pay for added features and aesthetics.

On the other hand, if you sell scientific test equipment and call on the same customers, you would segment very differently. Only a subset of schools is even in your addressable market; specifically, high schools or middle schools with chemistry labs. And the needs of hospitals would vary greatly based on size, location, and whether or not it is a teaching hospital. So you might imagine three or four different segments of hospitals with different tailored offerings and sales tactics for each.

Some Practical Tips for Segmenting

Remember that Grassroots Strategy is not a linear process. You cannot turn off your brain and fill in the blanks to get to a strategy. The same is true for the segmentation process. It takes a willingness to roll up your sleeves and dive in. And it takes experience to know when you've achieved "good enough" and when you should keep pushing for deeper insights.

Here are the basic steps in getting to a market segmentation:

1. **Define the "universe" you are segmenting.** Is it global or just Europe? What is its level in the value chain (distributor, installer, end customer)? What unit are you segmenting (application, building, automotive platform, parent company)? It may be necessary to segment at multiple levels to really understand your customer base. Sometimes one level is obviously the right choice and sometimes it is more difficult. But get this wrong and the rest of your work is for naught.

2. **Review your customer needs**, which should look a lot like value. If you have a good list of value elements, this is an opportunity to summarize and reword them. Focus on the differentiating needs, as points of parity are rarely good segmentation variables. And wherever possible, be careful not to use "ity" words to summarize complex customer trade-offs. We discuss them in Chapter 5 (Customer Value) as one of several traps in describing your value to B2B customers.

3. **Uncover discriminating needs.** What things do some customers need a lot of and some need a little? When you can describe these needs, ask yourself what's behind them (the "why"). Look for fundamental economic needs, not just behaviors. And keep in mind that a long list of needs is actually the enemy of good segmentation. You are looking for the critical few (usually no more than two or three) that really distinguish how the customer wants to be served differently.

4. **Propose a segmentation.** We like to call this step "and then a miracle occurs." Remember that a segmentation must match characteristics (demographics) to needs. This usually starts

with the insight, "this group of customers seems similar because..."

5. **Test the segmentation.** Create a table like we used in the truck parts example to ensure that the proposed segments are actually segments. The table should show that they have different needs, they can be identified by visible characteristics, that there is at least one real customer in the segment and most importantly, the implications for how you would serve them differently.

6. **Pick your target segments.** Based on your understanding of segment attractiveness, which segments do you want to target and with (roughly) what priority? Just as important, are there segments you want to avoid?

7. **Write value propositions** for your target segments. We will introduce a template in Chapter 7 (Value Proposition) but for now, quantify value in currency for each segment relative to their next best alternative.

8. **Gather actual customer data** to validate your hypotheses. Use Voice of the Customer and other techniques to test your assumptions and update the segmentation based on what you find. Do not overlook this step! The reasons will become clear when we get to Chapter 10 (Hypothesis Testing).

9. **Design segment-specific go-to-market plans** (and potentially different business models) to communicate and deliver your value propositions to the selected target segments.

10. **Implement the strategy** and put in place the changes in organization, business process, sales tactics, and measurements to make the strategy real.

Choosing Target Segments

We believe that key elements of market strategy are identifying and targeting the most attractive segments, investing in uniquely meeting their needs, and getting paid for the value you create. But how do you define segment attractiveness?

It's tempting to fall back on market data, especially around something tangible like unit volume. For all the reasons described in Chapter 3 (Market Definition and Opportunity), we believe that this is at best incomplete and at worst misleading.

As we learned in the dog food example, the temptation to quantify can lead to segmentation that although measurable, is not helpful. And it's important to remember that the only market you can measure exactly is last year's market for existing offerings. If you are considering offering something new or different, this may be only tangentially relevant.

Segment attractiveness cannot be reduced to a formula, although it is a function of segment size or opportunity, growth rate, willingness/ability to pay, and your ability to offer differential value. As we saw in the China truck aftermarket story earlier in this chapter, the most attractive segment depends on how you are differentiated. You would view the market quite differently, for example, if you were a Chinese company competing primarily on price.

Here's an example that makes this point vividly. Our client wanted to enter the Chinese market for energy management services. While this concept was relatively new to China, it was an established market in much of the world served by consultants, equipment makers and in some cases, utilities. The offering was to analyze a building's energy efficiency and make recommendations on how to run the building differently with a goal of saving energy. A common recommendation is replacing incandescent bulbs with LED bulbs. To varying degrees, these companies may also design and implement the proposed changes and even guarantee results.

Our client had been successful in other markets with a controls-based approach. That is, they didn't just look for one-time fixes. They used sensors and switches to monitor and control energy usage on an ongoing basis. Controls ensured that savings were actually realized by rapidly adjusting energy usage to match building usage (cutting off air conditioning on a vacant floor), for example, and preventing someone from resetting a thermostat during third shift.

When they looked at energy consumption in China, by far the biggest segment was process industries (steel, aluminum, beverage plants) that use huge amounts of energy. In fact, they already had a profitable contract with one of China's oldest breweries.

But when they looked at their ability to differentiate, process industries became less attractive.

Most needs are met with one-time changes to processes or equipment. There is little incremental value in monitoring and controls, since the basic operation is either on or off. In practical terms, the energy consumption of a steel mill is very high but is nearly constant on an hourly or daily basis.

Worse, because there is little investment required to make these recommendations beyond domain knowledge in the specific process industry, our client would likely have been competing with an army of retired process engineers selling themselves as consultants, sometimes at very low local rates. Finally, when they dug deeper, it turned out that the brewery contract was awarded based on political connections that were probably not repeatable.

Since our client's strength is a controls-based approach, an attractive segment would be one that most values its benefits, such as a segment whose buildings have variable usage. The more variable and unpredictable, the more important it becomes to use sensors and feedback systems instead of just turning the heat down at the same time every evening.

Easily identifiable vertical markets, such as hotels and schools, fall into this category. Energy usage varies throughout the year based on occupancy, and energy requirements vary with unique, one-time events, like a big wedding on Saturday or a basketball game on Tuesday night.

This more targeted strategy turned out to be a winner. Because they could more effectively target winning projects, the client closed several big deals based on value with a very small sales investment.

Summary

Let's review the key lessons from these segmentation stories from the consumer and B2B markets.

- Consider first what you're trying to segment. People often jump to the conclusion that they should segment their direct customer, or in the case of dog food, accept someone else's definition of the customer (the dog), when in fact a different kind of thinking would serve them better. Ask yourself who receives value from your product or offering and start there.

- Don't segment by product. Segment based on your differentiation and the broader customer needs, as illustrated with the dog food and truck parts examples.

- Don't fall into the trap of pushing your technology and losing sight of what the market actually wants. As the Skullcandy example tells us, segmentation is about needs and might have very little to do with technology, even if yours is exceptional. There are no "standard" or "premium" customers. Some pay for the higher-priced product because they have different needs.

- Don't change your segmentation to match your competitor's, even if they are succeeding where you are not. This will only lead to me-too products. Consider that the competitor's product may serve a different function and therefore a different segment, like *The New York Times* vs. *USA Today*. Whenever possible, base your segmentation on something that differentiates you, not what someone else is doing.

- Focus on all aspects of your offering. As the truck parts story shows, sometimes you can find latent needs that help you break out of the existing segmentation, especially if you look beyond the product (and don't accept someone else's segmentation).

- Establish a meaningful basis for segmentation. Meaningful implies there is different value in different segments that are actionable based on the way you service and price each segment.

- Identify segments in advance using data on customer characteristics, not sales data. You can't wait until after a customer buys to decide what segment they are in. You need to know their segment in order to develop and communicate the best offerings at the right prices. In consumer marketing this is often called a "typing study," which uses demographic or survey data to predict the likely segment for a potential customer. In B2B markets it can be far simpler, but it should not be subjective.

- Similarly, a segmentation scheme need not be perfect to be useful. Your predictions may be wrong sometimes, but as long as you build in the ability to learn over time, your segmentation scheme will improve. Let's say you sell medical equipment and have classified a certain hospital as an early adopter. But then when you visit, you find that every piece of equipment they own is at least ten years old. Clearly this hospital was placed in the wrong segment, but why?

  Perhaps the hospital was segmented based on incorrect information. If so, correct your data and move them to the appropriate segment. Or maybe the segmentation needs to be refined in some way. Whatever the situation, figure out why your prediction was wrong and learn from the experience.

- It is not always true that the biggest segment matters most. Segment size is just one measure. Unless you can create differentiation and thus value for all customers in that segment, you may be chasing the same segment as all your competitors, as did our client using building controls to sell energy savings.

Unlike value, which has one quantifiable answer, segmentation is a blend of art and science. There is no repeatable process that we guarantee will produce segmentation in a fixed amount of time.

It is messy and iterative and can even be confrontational. But we hope we have convinced you that, given the alternatives of not segmenting or segmenting incorrectly, segmentation is worth the effort.

Done well, segmentation is critical for a winning market-back strategy and can unlock previously untapped sources of growth and profit. But it must be implemented to have any effect. Segmentation is not finished until you have clearly defined the differences in approach you will use for each customer, based on their segment.

Lastly, we have a wonderfully circular definition, since customers in the same segment have similar needs, they want the same value proposition. So, as we define value proposition in the next chapter remember that we are always talking about something segment-specific.

7

Value Proposition

A lmost every company today talks about their "value proposition," but is everyone defining and using the phrase consistently? More to the point, what constitutes a "good" value proposition?

The phrase was coined in a paper titled, "A Business is a Value Delivery System." It was published in 1988 by the consulting firm McKinsey & Co., and authored by Michael Lanning and Edward Michaels (Lanning & Michaels, 1988). The paper defines a value proposition as "a clear, simple statement of the benefits, both tangible and intangible, that the company will provide, along with the approximate price it will charge each customer segment for those benefits."

That definition has evolved over the years and is now widely accepted to be "a promise of value to be delivered, communicated, and acknowledged." So, a value proposition informs how you communicate with potential customers through your marketing messaging and sales presentations. But that's not all. In our view, your value proposition is the foundation of how you engage customers and what you deliver to them.

The better way to define a value proposition is that it is the integration of all of your thinking developed through the framework until now: your target segment (and level of the value chain), your offering, and how you demonstrate and deliver differential value.

So, you need to ensure your value proposition is strategically actionable by asking and answering these questions:

- Why should a specific customer, with a certain set of needs in a unique segment, care about your offering?

- Do you fully understand and solve those needs?

- Why do you believe your offering will solve their needs better than any of their other options?

- Why is your offering priced as it is?

- Why should the customer choose your offering over their next best alternative?

- How is your offering differentiated?

- What do you actually do to achieve that differentiation?

- Why should the customer believe you?

Value Proposition Framework

A good value proposition should answer all of these questions. It should enable your messaging to move from "marketing fluff" to a customer promise that you can stand behind. The best value propositions articulate what is actually true, not what you hope customers will believe is true.

Geoffrey Moore's positioning statement from "Crossing the Chasm" (Moore, 1991) is the basis of our value proposition framework. After years of experience working with clients and delivering our Grassroots Strategy sessions, we have modified Moore's original statement and enhanced it with two additions: quantified value and proof points.

The resulting template reflects our emphasis on quantifying value and the importance of proof points for B2B customers. Some of our clients fondly refer to this template as the "Mad Libs" of Grassroots Strategy. Like the old-school children's game, you can tell a story after filling in the blanks.

For _____

(target customer/segment)

that need _____,

(the problem(s) we solve)

our _____

(the offering that you deliver)

provides _____

(quantified value)

unlike _____.

(the next best alternative)

We do this by _____

(how do we do it)

as demonstrated by _____.

(proof points)

Let's break down how this works together to create a value proposition.

Customer Segment

It starts with a target customer/segment. Customers are not all the same, so your value proposition must be specific to a group of customers with similar needs (segment) that value your offering in the same way. This has several implications.

First, it's unlikely your company will have only one value proposition unless you have only one offering that it sells to one customer segment. Second, each offering will have a value proposition for every customer segment you're targeting. And finally, if you're selling different offerings to the same customer segment, you may have multiple value propositions for that segment.

Next you clearly define the unique and differentiating needs of the customer segment. The operative word is "unique" because it is this set of needs that makes this customer segment different from all the others. It does not include universal customer needs. If you are selling an email system, the universal need for all customers is that the system be able to send and receive email. A unique differentiating need is that some customers need to send emails with very large file attachments, while others may not.

Offering

Now that you've defined who you are serving and identified their unique and differentiated needs, you will detail the "total offering" you intend to sell them. Notice we didn't say "product." As we have said elsewhere, the total offering includes the product as well as related services, terms and conditions, guarantees, and anything else that serves their unique needs in a differentiated way.

Quantified Customer Value

Here's where we get to the heart and soul of a value proposition, which is the value you create for your customer. This is one of the ideas we added to Moore's positioning statement.

Many value propositions fall short because they fail to quantify their value proposition in currency. Instead, they stop at descriptive benefits or worse yet, use vague marketing terms that are essentially meaningless.

Here's a quick recap from Chapter 5 (Customer Value) on the three rules for value:

1. It is customer (or segment) specific

2. It is quantified in currency (Dollars, Euros, RMB, Pounds, Rupees, etc.). Do not enter percentages or intangibles like "better quality" or "superior performance."

3. It is relative to the customer's next best alternative

This last rule of "next best alternative" is a critical yet often overlooked element of value. What else could the customer do besides purchase your total offering? They could do nothing and continue their current way of doing things, build an in-house solution to the problem, or buy from your competitor.

You need to be completely honest and ask yourself, "If I were the customer, what else could I be doing?" If they are not yet comparing you to these alternatives, you can bet they soon will be.

Source of Differentiation

Understanding customer value requires a clear understanding of differentiation. Your value proposition needs to explain what creates this differentiation. So, you need to ask yourself:

- What do you do that is unique and different from other alternatives that helps your customer solve specific problems in a way that creates value for them?

- What makes your offering special in a way that matters to the customer?

Again, be completely honest. Describe the most important differentiators that are actually true, not those you would like the customer to believe are true. This is no place for the advertising puffery so common in consumer marketing: "Drink this beer and it will change your life!" Rather, this is where you explain to the buyer(s) how you create value that no one else can. Remember they might have to justify to their boss why they are spending more up front for the value you deliver.

This is also where you communicate to others in your organization what everyone needs to focus on to win. So, something like, "Our patented hydraulic technology delivers better fuel efficiency saving you $1,500 per year over the life of the motor" may not be sexy, but it is perfectly acceptable.

Proof Points

The final component is proof, which is especially difficult for new offerings. This is another addition we made to Moore's positioning statement.

How can you demonstrate to a prospective customer that what you are saying is actually true? Should you:

- Perform field trials or pilots to gather evidence?

- Use a third party to test your offerings against the next best alternative?

- Include a guarantee of performance?

- Create case studies using reference customers that are already convinced of your value?

- Deploy sales tools like value calculators and ROI tools that allow customers to estimate the value themselves?

You need to do whatever it will take to convince a skeptical customer that they should invest in your offering. No decision maker or CFO will commit to your solution unless they believe it will create more value and have a positive impact on their business. Remember, proof points have to link to your differentiation. They are not what qualifies you to be in the business, they are the evidence that you can create better outcomes for the customer. In other words, "decades of industry experience" is not a proof point.

To summarize, a value proposition is an internal declaration of your marketing strategy. And while it should inform your marketing communications, it is not meant to be your sales pitch. A good value proposition is built around clear differentiation, an understanding of the relevant next best alternative, quantification of value, and compelling proof.

This is the first and only place in the book where we encourage you to use a template. This is by design. Too often, templates are an excuse to turn off the brain and fill in the blanks. They're easy, but this template is not. You must be confident that every part of your value proposition is true to the best of your knowledge. You are likely to find that filling in the last four blanks will prove to be quite challenging. Done well, test driving the value proposition from the customer's perspective is what makes it compelling.

Case Study: Packaging Material

We once worked with a client on building a value proposition for a packaging material that was struggling to gain traction in the market. The details are disguised, but the overall story is true.

This packaging material was an ultraviolet light (UV) barrier film that could be adhered as a layer in a PVC-based package. Because the film was clear, it had the dual benefits of protecting the contents of the package from UV exposure while keeping the contents visible.

One target application was sensitive electronics components, which were typically packaged at the time using aluminum foil. The advantage of transparent film is that it simplified incoming inspection to the component manufacturer's customer.

However, although the film is a good UV barrier, it is not as good as aluminum foil. And it costs five to ten times more than aluminum foil, and is only one layer in the package.

The business team had tried for almost three years to penetrate this market without much success. We discovered that they had focused on selling the advantages of clear film to packaging engineers and purchasing managers. These decision makers had little appreciation for the benefits of clear film because they were primarily tasked with finding the least expensive packaging material to protect the components during shipment.

Their messaging and approach at the time might have led to a sales call like this.

Sales Rep: We have this great new packaging film that can protect your product from UV radiation. And it can help you brand your products and reduce your customers' incoming inspection costs.

Customer: We use aluminum foil today and it is works great. How does it compare to aluminum as a UV barrier?

Sales Rep: Well, it's almost as good as aluminum and we find that most of the time, it's good enough.

Customer: Okay, so it isn't as good as aluminum. How much does it cost?

Sales Rep: It is $8 per square meter.

Customer: Are you kidding? We're paying $1 per square meter for aluminum. *(At this point, the customer is annoyed and ready to end the meeting)*

Sales Rep: Yes, but we can help achieve higher sales and lower your customers' incoming inspection costs.

Customer: My job is to deliver good products at the lowest possible packaging cost. This meeting is over!

It's not hard to see why they were struggling to grow sales. During our Grassroots Strategy session with this team, we explored all the differentiated benefits that their material had over aluminum. One that quickly emerged was the product density that could be achieved with their material versus aluminum.

With aluminum, you need to place the components very far apart or the aluminum will crack or tear. With their material, you could package two to three times the number of components in the same amount of material. And, since this is only one layer in a package with secondary packaging, and since these components were packaged on very expensive packaging lines using a lot of energy and labor, the total packaging cost with aluminum was actually quite high.

In the end, the total cost of packaging with our client's material was almost always cheaper, even at five to ten times the price per square meter. The value proposition was strong, even without including the benefits around growing sales and reducing customer inspection cost.

Using the framework presented earlier in this chapter, here is the client's value proposition for this target segment.

For *large integrated electronic component manufacturers*

(target customer/segment)

that need *to reduce the total cost of packaging,*

(the problem(s) we solve)

our *UVX 1000 Barrier and re-designed packaging solution*

(the offering that you deliver)

provides *$1 million savings per $5 million of components shipped*

(quantified value)

unlike *the current aluminum foil packaging.*

(the next best alternative)

We do this by *increasing component package density*

(how do we do it)

as demonstrated by *beta tests with key customers.*

(proof points)

With this insight, the team began refining their go-to-market strategy. They developed value-based messaging, value calculators, and ROI tools, and used case studies to demonstrate the value their packaging material delivered.

Within a year, the client went from less than $1 million in sales in this market to a $30 million run-rate and became the packaging material of choice for eight of the top ten electronic component manufacturers.

Operationalizing Your Value Proposition

Once you have one or more segment-level value propositions for your offering, what do you do with them?

Your value proposition(s) should form the basis of what everyone in your company does as it relates to that customer segment. Think of it as the guidebook or standard operating procedure for how you serve that segment of customers. If the value proposition is your promise to customers, you had better make sure you have the ability to actually deliver on that promise. This is why we encourage our clients to teach these concepts to cross-functional teams. No matter how good the thinking, you can't win if the ideas never leave the marketing department.

Let's look at how a value proposition directly impacts the activities of four functional areas.

R&D / Product Development

The value proposition of your highest priority segments should guide the development of new offerings as well as enhancements to or removal of features from current offerings. Everything in the offering roadmap should focus on enhancing the value proposition(s) for one or more of your target segments.

Roadmap items should be prioritized by how much value they create for your customer segments. If a new feature or enhancement can't be linked to creating more value for one or more target segments, it should be removed from the roadmap. If you are missing a feature that's keeping you from winning in a target segment (we called that type of value element a P-), then that should be on your roadmap as well.

Operations

Performance metrics and priorities should be tied to the value propositions of your targeted customer segments. These specifications should be well understood by everyone in operations and should always be met. Here's how that might work.

Let's assume that a key part of your value proposition for a priority segment is delivering on time, and that delivery time is less important for other segments. Rather than risk missing a delivery for the priority segment, customers in that segment should always be bumped up in the production queue to ensure meeting their expectations every time. No exceptions!

Marketing

All messaging should be specific to each segment and should reflect the value proposition for that segment. Your website and marketing collateral should be designed to target, guide, and communicate your value proposition effectively to each target segment.

Pricing for each target segment should be established based on the value proposition for that group of customers. And, sales tools should enable the sales team to qualify a prospective customer into a target segment, and then effectively communicate the value proposition for that target segment.

Sales

It goes without saying that your value propositions matter a lot to sales. This should be the basis of who they target, how they talk to them, and how they win their business.

There are two big challenges for sales. First, they need to develop the discipline to walk away from customers that aren't in a target segment. Second, they need to understand that pricing is based on the value delivered to the customer (based on segment), and not based on volume or whom they like best.

When multiple segments buy the same product, one way to achieve the value of segmentation is to offer different service levels for different prices. A large customer base might even self-select from a menu of services, much like you might choose to pay more for express shipping when you have waited until the last minute to order your spouse's birthday gift.

In addition to R&D, operations, marketing, and sales, every other department in your organization is impacted by your value propositions. Accounting and finance need to measure performance by segment, not some other arbitrary cut of customers. HR needs to understand the skills and talents that are most critical for delivering your value propositions, and how the skills needed potentially vary by segment. Customer service needs to know which customers should always be prioritized, and which need to pay up front to receive support.

Always strive to make sure that every department or functional area is organized and measured appropriately to ensure that you can consistently deliver your value proposition to all target segments.

Three Levels of a Value Proposition

You already know that a separate value proposition is needed for every offering and for every target segment of customers. But that's not all.

Although we use segmentation to group customers based on a common set of needs, that doesn't mean all customers in a segment are exactly the same. Why? Because value is customer specific.

Each individual customer within a segment has a specific set of circumstances that makes them unique. They are generally more similar to other customers in that segment than to customers in another segment, but they're not exactly the same.

To make matters more complex, consider that company decisions are really made by individuals. Thus, you also need to account for the individual roles and motivations of the people involved in the decision-making process.

Even within a given customer segment, you ultimately have three distinct versions of your value proposition: segment, company, and role.

Segment
- What customer segments do you want to target?
- How would customers within the segment describe their issues and needs?
- How would they articulate the quantified benefits your solution can deliver versus the competition?

Company
- In what specific ways will company revenues be increased and costs reduced as a result of this new solution?
- What are the strategic benefits associated with introducing this new solution?
- Do we have customer evidence to support the business benefit claims?

Role
- Which key individuals will be involved in making or influencing the buying decision?
- What are their roles, responsibilities and key challenges your solution can address?
- How will they perceive personal value associated with your solution?

Here's how these three levels work together. Marketing owns the segment-level value propositions and is responsible for ensuring that everyone else understands them. Sales owns the role-level value propositions, since their activities focus on the different roles within the buying process (technical, financial, blocker, approver, user, etc.).

Typically, marketing should provide a framework or mechanism that converts the segment-level value proposition into a company-level value proposition for each target customer in the segment. In general, the sources of value are the same within a segment, but the magnitude of the value will likely differ depending on company size and other factors.

Sometimes it is helpful to think that marketing owns the segment-level value proposition and sales is responsible for converting it into a customer-specific business case. This takes a combination of tools and training.

Training should focus on helping the sales team shift from selling the features and functions of your offering to selling the value it delivers, which is supported by specific features and functions. But, to truly enable your sales team to sell based on value, you need to provide them with sales tools designed for that purpose.

These tools need to help your sales team do the following:

1. Assess and fully understand the needs of the prospect (assessment tools)

2. Ask the right questions to determine the value your offering could create for a specific customer (value calculators)

3. Build a business case (formally for major project sales) to cost-justify your proposal and help your sponsor sell your solution internally (ROI tools)

All three tools may not always be necessary, but you will likely be much more successful if sales has these tools available to build a compelling business case for each specific customer.

Value Proposition Evolution

Often when our clients reach this point, they realize that they're creating so much value for their customers that they should be capturing more of it. And they are absolutely right! However, we believe that with value-based pricing and value sharing, several steps need to occur before you can be confident in that approach.

We created a framework for thinking about the evolution of a value proposition from cost or market-based pricing to value pricing or value sharing.

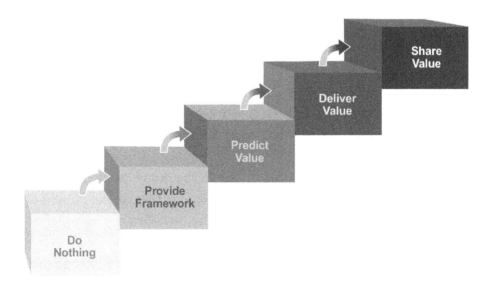

- **Do Nothing.** Needless to say, this is the worst place to be. You can only react to competitive prices and you are at the whim of your customer.

- **Provide Value Framework.** By providing your customer with a framework that shows how you create value for them, you can discuss and justify your price relative to the competition. That's helpful, but not enough. You are still left at the mercy of your customer understanding the framework and applying it correctly to determine the value that you provide.

- **Predict Value.** This is where you use your framework to develop tools that predict the value your offering could provide to your customers. This requires a deep understanding of your customers' business and a sales process that leverages that understanding.

- **Ensure Value Realization.** Now that you've predicted and persuaded the customer that you can help them make more money (value), you need to actually deliver that value. This can often be more challenging than one might think. Many things can prevent a customer from realizing the predicted value: poor implementation, lack of training, lack of adoption, misalignment with business processes, missing features and functionality, or simply lack of monitoring and measuring performance. It takes constant diligence to ensure that customers are actually receiving the promised value.

First, your offering must truly solve the entire problem and meet their needs. Next, you must ensure that the solution is deployed properly. This can take the form of a professional services delivery capability and/or a qualified partner network or strong customer service. Finally, any significant change in a business requires a combination of people, process, and tools.

Make sure that the people impacted by your solution are properly trained. If your solution requires changes in the way people do their jobs, you might need to assist them with business processes, tools, and appropriate metrics for performance. Bottom line, you are not done until the customer realizes and acknowledges the economic returns promised in your value proposition.

- **Share Value.** Value sharing is the most enticing, yet dangerous level in the pricing evolution framework. Before you attempt value sharing, you must have already nailed the previous levels: value framework, value prediction, and value delivery. Otherwise, you are highly likely to fail.

  It's not enough to successfully deliver a lot of value to one customer. If you don't want to lose money, you must also understand the underlying value drivers before you attempt value sharing with another customer. We very much favor pricing your offering relative to the value that you provide, as described in Chapter 8 (Value Pricing). But we have seen far too many gain-sharing schemes fail, so proceed with caution.

This framework does not imply that the goal is always to get to the top step. Sometimes value sharing is too complex or is unacceptable to the customer. Even where value sharing is not feasible, it can be helpful to think about pricing in this way, as it forces you to truly understand the customer's perspective.

A related and important lesson from Chapter 5 (Customer Value) is that the more value you create, the more you can invest in creating new business models and pricing mechanisms to capture it. For example, you might be able to charge per unit of customer's output or shift to a subscription fee rather than a standard per item sold price.

Managing your Value Proposition

Once you have written and communicated your value proposition, you should engrave it on a plaque, hang it in everyone's office, and move on to other activities, right? Not so fast.

Value propositions are living documents that should be continually reevaluated and updated as things change. Some changes are good; some not so good. Let's start with the good reasons.

An obvious reason for reevaluating your value proposition is that R&D, engineering, and offering development efforts have effectively improved how you solve specific customer needs. By increasing your differentiation, these efforts increase the value you deliver to customers.

A more subtle reason for reevaluating your value proposition is that because your entire organization has been doing whatever is necessary to deliver your value proposition, you continue to improve your ability to deliver on that promise. The more you do it, the better you become, and the harder it is for a competitor to catch up. This is a flywheel business model, which we will discuss at length in Chapter 9 (Business Model).

Another benefit of actively managing your value proposition is the opportunity to eliminate activities that distract you from optimizing your delivery. As you align your entire business model around delivering on your value proposition, your company becomes a well-oiled machine that's hard to compete with. And as your customer's situation and economics improve, you gain even more advantages over your competition. Again, more on this in Chapter 9 (Business Model).

Unfortunately, if you discover more negative factors than positive, it's definitely time to reevaluate your value proposition. Let's start with the most obvious, the next best alternative.

Despite your best efforts, your competitors are always working to improve their offerings and reduce your differentiation. Over time most things will be copied, which reduces your value delivered when compared to the next best alternative. And, the more value you create and capture, the more incentive there is for customers, competitors, and new players to find or develop an alternative solution.

While most companies spend at least some time tracking direct competitors, it is also a good idea to periodically review "not in kind" alternatives. Changes in factors like technology, price, or infrastructure may change the next best alternative. You may not always be able to catch disruptive changes, like Uber in the taxi market, but you should at least look for threats so that it's not too late to make changes when you recognize them.

Other factors that could impact your value proposition include regulations, disruptions in your customer's business model, changes in your customer's markets, innovative new products or technologies, and changes in market drivers.

The bottom line is that you must constantly evaluate and monitor all factors that could impact your value proposition so you can update and respond accordingly before you are negatively affected.

Value Proposition Traps

The most common trap is thinking that your value proposition is all about marketing spin. In fact, your value proposition should be a statement of your strategy to win and deliver value to a particular customer segment. Although it is the basis for your marketing message, you will ultimately fail if you don't have a strategy to make your value proposition customer promise true over time.

We also see lists of attributes, ratings, and features masquerading as value propositions. Although you need differentiated sets of capabilities and features to have a compelling value proposition, what matters is how the entire offering creates value.

While we might sound repetitious, we continue to be surprised by how often we see marketing spin masquerading as a value proposition. By diligently and objectively applying this framework from the customer's perspective, you can avoid the following traps when developing your value proposition:

- Making it generic instead of segment-specific, or worse, about your company not about the customer

- Listing the features or benefits of your product instead of translating those features to customer value

- Choosing the wrong next-best-alternative for the segment

- Failing to understand your 'burden of proof' from the customer's perspective and knowing what you need to demonstrate to convince them

- Thinking that your value proposition is cast in stone and not reevaluating it periodically

- Not institutionalizing your value proposition to ensure that the entire organization is aligned with delivering its promise

When done correctly, a value proposition can be a great test of your strategy. It requires understanding the customer's problem, quantifying the value of the problem, and segmenting the market based on needs. Only then you can align the organization to deliver on each and every value proposition.

Summary

A value proposition is an essential component of any good B2B marketing strategy, and it is far more than just a marketing message. A solid value proposition should:

- Identify who you are targeting (segment)

- Distinguish which specific needs you serve better than any other solutions

- Describe your total offering for that segment of customers

- Quantify how much value it creates for customers in that segment

- Identify the next-best alternatives against which you will be compared

- Describe how you are going to solve the customers' problems

- Demonstrate how you are going to prove it

If you can confidently answer all of these questions, then you have a greater chance of success.

Every offering and every target customer segment needs its own value proposition. Those value propositions should serve as the roadmap for all parts of the organization so they can deliver on them every day.

Once you have a solid value proposition, you can move on to the next step and the next chapter: setting your price to capture the value created by your offering.

8

Value Pricing

There is an old story about value pricing we like to share. A new optometrist just starting his practice seeks advice from his father, who is also an optometrist. He tells his father that he learned a lot in school, but that they didn't teach how to price eyeglasses. "How do you know how much to charge?"

His father replies, "Son, that's easy. When someone asks how much their glasses will cost, you tell them $100. If they don't react, you say for the frames. And the lenses will be another $100. If they still don't react, you say each."

This simple anecdote shows that different buyers will pay different prices for your offering and the price they are willing to pay is based on the value they expect to receive. But customers rarely tell you how much value they expect to receive directly. Nor will they tell you how much they are really willing to pay.

The Goal of Pricing

Although B2B pricing isn't as simple as our story, its goal is crystal clear and three-fold:

1. To maximize the earnings your company receives…

2. Over the life of the offering…

3. Based on the value it delivers to your customers.

Have you ever had a customer tell you that your price is too low? Probably not. Customers want more for less every day. They will, however, tell you that you are overpriced. Does that necessarily mean that your offering is actually overpriced? Maybe, but probably not. The true test is whether they pay the price that you offer. If they do, then your offering is not overpriced no matter how much they complain.

Your job is to maximize your offering's profitability and return on investment for your company. That's a huge responsibility! If you price incorrectly, the best-case scenario is you make the sale but leave money on the table. The worst case is you lose a sale you could have won, thereby losing the contribution margin that could have come from that deal.

If pricing is so critical, why do most companies arbitrarily choose a generic pricing strategy instead of always setting the profit-maximizing price? The answer is simple. It's very easy to label your pricing approach and just hand out a price list. It's a lot harder to figure out the optimal price for your offerings.

There are many online resources that tout their top-ten pricing models and Wikipedia lists a whopping 26 different pricing models or strategies. In reality, all pricing strategies can be grouped into one of four broad categories: cost-based, market-based, psychological-based, and value-based.

Cost-Based Pricing

This strategy uses the cost to produce and deliver an offering as the basis for calculating its price. And, to be blunt, it's lazy. It's much easier to calculate your cost to deliver the offering than it is to understand what a customer should be willing to pay it. Examples of cost-based pricing include absorption pricing, marginal cost pricing, contribution margin pricing and cost-plus pricing.

If you are using cost-based pricing in any form, **STOP NOW!**

Cost-based pricing strategies masquerade in many forms. After a pricing discussion during a Grassroots Strategy session, a participant told us, "Wow, great stuff! I'm happy to say we don't do cost-based pricing. We do target-margin pricing." When we asked how they calculate their target margin, he hesitated and admitted, "Oh, it's a target margin over our cost."

Any pricing model that uses your cost as an input is a poor pricing strategy. We used to say that cost-plus pricing was the worst form of pricing that exists. That was until we learned of instances where the costs weren't well understood to begin with, and they ended up with cost-minus pricing. Both are bad, but I think we can agree that cost-minus pricing is even worse! If you are losing money on each sale, you can't make it up in volume.

Fluctuating costs make cost-based pricing even more impractical. If your costs go down, you might be tempted to lower your prices or be more willing to negotiate if a customer insists on a discount. And when your costs go up, good luck increasing your prices along with them! Even if your customers agree to pay more for your offering due to a price increase in a major ingredient (say the price of oil), know that they will ask for a price reduction when the price of that ingredient goes down.

If you still think cost-based pricing is a good idea, consider that very few companies know their actual cost to serve a given customer. You'll likely end up pricing based on your average cost and letting customers self-select instead of targeting those for whom you create the most value. This leaves you vulnerable to competitors that do a better job segmenting the market.

In our work, we have come across situations where a cost-based strategy led to prices that seemed fair but were capturing only a fraction of the value created. In some cases, the prices were too low by a factor of more than ten!

So, if cost-based pricing is so obviously wrong, why does it persist?

- It's **simple.** Understanding customer value takes work and is an ongoing, time-consuming process. By comparison, costs and target margins are based on history and are generally dictated by finance.

- It's **precise** (even if it is precisely wrong). Value is an ever-changing estimate whereas accountants can usually calculate the cost to produce your offering (CoGS) to within three or four decimal places. Although this precision may provide some comfort, it is misleading because it is usually based on last year's average cost, not the current total cost to serve any specific customer.

- It **seems fair.** Value is usually derived from product features or service benefits that took many years to build and strengthen. The cost of this investment is relatively invisible to customers. Tacking a "reasonable" margin onto current costs seems easier to defend, especially when customers are facing a profitability challenge themselves.

- It's **internally focused.** Value puts price in the context of what we could charge versus the next best alternative, but this requires external research to understand. Internal benchmarks are far simpler: our typical margins are 35% and we priced this new product at 40%, which must be good, right?

Cost-based pricing is like weeds in your garden. Without constant diligence, it will keep coming back. The only way to permanently shift internal dialogue from cost to value is to cultivate a broad awareness of strategic marketing principles.

There is only one circumstance in which cost-based pricing can be unavoidable. Some government contracts explicitly demand cost-plus pricing, at least in the short term. Our experience tells us that there are usually options in the long run. And if you can show that your offering is available commercially-off-the-shelf (CoTS), you can often price your offering at market prices, even with government contracts.

Sometimes government contracts have bonus clauses or make additional margin available based on performance, which is a direct way of pricing based on value. Even when these are absent, most contracts include some ability to negotiate which costs can be included, which is an indirect way of pricing to value. As government budgets fall under increased scrutiny, there may be an opportunity to move to market-based pricing, which is far simpler, administratively, and likely better for everyone involved.

Lastly, if you are pricing based on cost, you are playing into the hands of your customers' purchasing managers. Recall our discussion of 'should cost' models in Chapter 5 (Customer Value).

One of our clients sold turbochargers to major vehicle manufacturers. A customer informed them one day that they had torn down their product, weighed the individual components, looked up the prices for the specific alloys, and determined what their turbocharger should cost. Not surprisingly, the figure was about one-third of what our client was currently charging.

Armed with an understanding of value, our client politely informed their customer that they were not just buying pounds of metal. To paraphrase their response, "Our turbochargers simultaneously push the limits of metallurgy, aerodynamics, and thermodynamics as engines run hotter to pursue both better fuel efficiency and lower emissions. We have enabled this performance while improving our quality to single-digit failures per million vehicles. In short, you are buying the accumulated engineering expertise that knows which materials to use for which parts and how to machine, assemble, and test them to maintain these increasingly high standards. If you think you can buy metal alloys less expensively than we can, we welcome that assistance and would be happy to pass along the savings. Otherwise, we stand by our price."

Their customer was silent and presumably not very happy, as purchasing managers are generally evaluated on cost savings. But in the end, our client kept the business without lowering their price. To restate the point that we hope is now obvious, this would not have been possible if they were pricing based on cost.

Market-Based Pricing

Market-based pricing is when you base your price on competing products in your marketplace. This is easy to do because you often know, at least roughly, what your competitors charge, they know what you charge, and so do potential customers. Sales-driven organizations sometimes call this the "price to win," as in, "If I can match competitor X at $120 per ton, then I can get this order."

This strategy makes the most sense in a true commodity market where customers base their buying decisions exclusively on price. If your offering is exactly the same as the competition, including everything in it that creates value, then your price must match others in the same market. But that's rarely the case in a B2B environment.

Market-based pricing strategies include skimming, penetration, predatory, premium, and price leadership. Basically what these have in common is that they benchmark our desired price to some industry price average or index. Although any of these may work, you must be careful not to leave money on the table. These may be better than simply matching market prices, but without a link to value, there is no way to know if you are pricing optimally.

Say you choose a price-skimming strategy and price your offering at a 10% premium. How do you know if 10% is the right premium? Could it have been 20%, 50%, or even 500%? Or should you have gone with 5%?

Likewise, with a penetration strategy. Pricing your product at 20% below the current market price may help you gain market share, but how do you know if 20% is the right amount? Will your discounted price trigger a price war if competitors slash their prices? Most importantly, if your offering delivers more value, should you use a premium pricing strategy instead?

We had one client who was running out of capacity for a major product line, so they launched a price increase of 10% across the board. Although the sales force grumbled and there were some uncomfortable conversations with purchasing managers, in the end they did not lose a single customer. They declared the program a success, and began to think of value pricing as a major capability.

In truth, all they demonstrated was that they were underpricing previously and with no understanding of value, they were surely leaving money on the table. There may have been segments of customers who would have paid 20%, 50%, or 200% more.

Basing your price on a percentage premium or discount off a competitor's price is a common but less informed approach. While it's important to consider competitor pricing when setting your own, it's only one factor among many. To avoid selling yourself short, we strongly recommend against using a market-based pricing strategy unless it incorporates the value of your offering to customers.

Psychological-Based Pricing

Psychological-based pricing is more prevalent in B2C markets, but it is slowly finding its way into B2B markets as well. The goal of these pricing schemes is to either trick buyers into acquiring something they don't need or hook them with a low price and then raise the price over time. Some of these methods can work quite effectively, even in B2B markets.

For example, the Freemium model is sometimes an effective psychological-based strategy. This is where you give away a free or limited version of your product (often software) and hold back many of the features that make the product really valuable. If you give the user enough functionality to encourage adoption or expand usage, some subset of customers may be willing to pay for the full or premium version of the offering.

The downside is that you don't gain any insight into how much the customer would have paid outright for the fully functional offering. In our experience, the Freemium model is a promotional and marketing strategy, not a pricing strategy. A legitimate pricing strategy establishes how much you charge paying customers, not how to hook them on your product.

Time-sensitive pricing is another example of psychological-based pricing. Although telling someone to "act now" to get a discount might work with consumers, business customers are more sophisticated than that. They know that if price discounting is available, they can expect to receive it whenever they decide to move forward with the purchase.

B2B customers have well-defined buying processes and use procurement agents that avoid responding to psychological-based pricing schemes. Consumers may think $199.99 is a better price than $200.00, but professional agents know that, for all intents and purposes, they are exactly the same.

Psychological pricing schemes are rarely effective over time in B2B markets. If you use one of these pricing mechanisms, you should first understand what customers are willing to pay so your pricing optimizes profitability. That can't happen unless you understand the value advantage your product delivers.

Value-Based Pricing

The goal of value-based pricing is to **leverage the value that your offering creates for customers** in order to **maximize its earnings impact** on your company. Easy, right? Unfortunately, it is much harder than it sounds.

Let's be absolutely clear about this. The goal is not to maximize the price you charge or the margin or profitability of a specific product. The goal is to maximize the earnings impact of the offering on the company.

Consider these factors to make sure you reap the full benefits of value-based pricing.

Optimal vs. Higher Prices

Will a higher price lead to higher profits? Maybe, but certainly not always. Basic economics tells us that a higher price has the potential to lower market demand, thus reducing sales and negatively impacting revenue.

Also consider whether your offering is easy to replicate and how well it is protected through patents and other forms of intellectual property protection. If inadequate protections are in place, high prices will create an incentive for competitors to copy what you've done and sell it at a lower price.

Even if your offering is well protected, a high price may encourage your customers to develop an alternative way to solve their problem. Remember, the goal of value pricing is to determine the optimal price to impact your earnings, which is not necessarily the highest price.

The Importance of a Balanced Approach

Maximizing profitability is a nuanced endeavor. If your company has more than one offering, it is important not to tweak the profitability of any one offering in a vacuum. You must consider how every pricing decision impacts the sale of other offerings.

If you charge a high price with a high margin for a new offering, you may be perceived as taking advantage of your position with existing customers. Even if they buy the new offering at the price you set, they may choose to take their business for other less differentiated offerings elsewhere. Is the margin from the new offering enough to offset the potential loss of other business?

Value based pricing focuses on maximizing the earnings impact across your entire business, not a specific product line. Keep this in mind when considering how to increase your margins.

Poorly Implemented Value-Based Pricing

Value-based pricing does not come without hazards. There are three pitfalls that can jeopardize future sales, customer satisfaction and of course, your bottom line.

- **Pitfall #1:**
  Choosing maximum price over optimum price.

  A previous discussion on market size and share emphasizes the importance of considering how your pricing might impact current customers. If a higher price no longer delivers comparable value, you risk losing future sales to competitors or in-house solutions. The optimum price is one that yields the most earnings while providing high value to your customers.

- **Pitfall #2:**
  Not re-evaluating your value position and pricing over time.

  The goal of pricing, and especially value pricing, is to maximize the earnings impact of your offering on your business. And every pricing model is based on multiple variables that are interdependent and vary over time. Your goal is to maximize profitability over the life of the offering. If you don't revisit these variables and reassess the value you provide, your pricing can alienate current and future customers.

- **Pitfall #3:**
  Using only average customer value to set prices.

  Too often, companies spend significant effort developing list prices and discount structures, but fail to fully understand the mechanisms that set prices for individual customers. One of the key differences between B2B and B2C marketing is that within reason, B2B allows you to set different prices by customer or customer segment.

Vary Prices by Segment

Value pricing is an art form, not a science. One reason is the sheer number of factors that goes into how much you can actually vary prices by customer. In general, we think that companies should push harder to vary prices to maximize profitability.

Concerns about customers talking to one another or comparing prices usually reflect an internal sense of what seems fair, which is not necessarily linked to the realities of customer behavior. We believe there is enormous flexibility in how to price discriminate, especially if you can vary service levels or other characteristics of your offering.

But Don't Go Too Far

That said, it is possible to go too far in optimizing price by individual customer. While we are big advocates of using value-based selling tools to help customers estimate the value of solving a problem, if a customer thinks the information they provided was used to set their specific price, you are likely to have a problem. Even if they follow through with the purchase, they are likely to look elsewhere for their next purchase.

When setting prices, you should absolutely use market information about customers and segments. But tricking individual customers into giving you information that is not public in order to set their price is not a good strategy. The only exception is if you are willing to enter into a value-sharing agreement, where you take some of the risk and share in the upside.

Calculating the Optimal Price

Now you understand **the risks of other pricing models** and how value pricing leverages the value your offering creates for customers to **maximize earnings for your company**. In a perfect world, the optimal price for a given customer could be calculated based on a limited set of variables. If you have taken any calculus, or at least some algebra, it is theoretically possible to figure it out.

Keep in mind that many of the critical variables are difficult to estimate, so it's not always practical to use this strictly as a formula. You will rarely have perfect information to populate the equation, but that shouldn't stop you from trying. What's important is that you understand why these variables are important, and how they factor into value pricing decisions.

Grappling with Value Pricing Variables

Settle in with your team and start discussing the inputs that go into the equation. Although it's difficult and may even be overwhelming, it's your responsibility. Taking shortcuts is sometimes successful in the short term but to succeed in the long run, you need to monitor these variables all the time.

- **The price of the next best alternative.** This is often a competitor, but it could be any alternative way that the customer can solve the problem. If their next best alternative is to **continue doing what they are doing today**, then the price of that alternative is $0.

- **The value that you create for the customer.** Quantify value in terms of **cost savings, improved efficiency, sales growth,** and any other way your offering can impact your customer's business.

- **The value that the next best alternative creates for the customer.** This is crucial. You can't price to capture more than the incremental value you create for your customer compared to their next best alternative.

- **The size of the market.** How big is the total market in terms of value created across all potential customers?

- **The market share that you expect to achieve at a given price.** This is dependent on your market reach, your competitor's likely response, and your **customer's price sensitivity** as well as the overall market's price elasticity. In other words, how much would total market demand change if market prices changed?

- **How long the offering will be in the market.** In years, what is the expected life of this offering?

- **The profitability you are already receiving from customers that could buy this offering.** Finally, you need to consider how much current profit could be at risk with those same customers. If you're launching a new offering in a market where you're already making a lot of money from those customers, you need to understand how your pricing decisions on the new offering could impact their buying decision on your other offerings.

As you work through these factors, keep in mind that they all change over time. Your goal isn't to maximize profitability for a single year, but over the life of the offering.

Further, as we will see below, many of these variables are interdependent. Bottom line, this is complex and there are a lot of factors that go into calculating your optimal price.

An Equation for the Ages

In a nutshell, here's what the value pricing equation accomplishes:

- It sets a price to maximize profitability over the N year life of your offering,

- Based on setting a price (which can vary over time) that captures a portion of the value delivered relative to the next best alternative, and

- Achieves a share of demand that delivers marginal contribution to the business when considering any product line cross interactions.

If you think that was rough, here's what it looks like using a mathematical equation. Warning! If you don't like math, you can skip this part.

$$\text{Maximize } (y=1 \text{ to } N \text{ Profit} = \sum(Pn(y) + V(y) * \mathbf{Cv(y)} - CoGS(y)) * M(y) * Sd(y) + Eo(y))$$

And here's how to interpret the variables in the equation where "y" represents year:

N	The life of the offering in years
Pn	Price of the Next Best Alternative in each year
V	Value your offering creates for the customer in each year relative to the Next Best Alternative
Cv	Percentage (%) of the value that is captured in the price (this is what you are solving for)
M	Unit-based market size in each year
Sd	Share of demand in each year (%)
Eo	Earnings impact on other offerings based on the price in each year

Then you solve for Cv by year to maximize profit. Simple, right?

The problem is that all of the variables are interdependent on both the price (share of value that you choose to capture) and each other. For instance, choosing a high percentage of value to capture (and thus a high price) could encourage new competing offerings (including customers choosing to do it themselves), which will in turn lower your share of demand and potentially the value that your offering creates vs. the next best alternative.

And, if you are selling other things to the same customers, that high price could cause those customers to stop buying other things from you, thus lowering the profit received from your other offerings.

In reality, these factors are virtually impossible to know with any level of confidence. But if you don't try to estimate the likely impact of each of them on various pricing decisions, you are likely to sub-optimize the earnings that your company will gain from your offering.

A More Practical Guide to Value Pricing

So, calculating the optimal price for your offering is theoretically possible but as you can see, it is practically impossible. There is a silver lining, though. By focusing on a few key factors, you can estimate the optimal price with some level of confidence.

These are the factors that need to be evaluated in your pricing decisions:

- Competitor response
- Price sustainability
- Cost structure
- Market size and share

To help you benefit from your pricing decisions, let's look at some of the most important factors that need to be evaluated.

The Competition

How will the competition likely respond to your pricing? Will they follow your lead or undercut your price?

If a competitor has a significantly lower cost structure, you need to evaluate whether they are likely to lower prices because they know they can remain profitable at lower prices than you and use it to their advantage. When you set your price, take into account how much you believe they can lower their price and still be comfortable.

If a competing product is either a significant part of their business or a loss-leader to sell other products, be ready for their response and price accordingly. If, however, you deliver considerably more value, and that value is far more than the amount that they can lower their price, you can be less concerned about their price reaction.

Alternatively, if you are considered the premium supplier, and thus the price leader, you can set a price point to capture a significant amount of the value, and your competitors may follow. This is especially true with new offerings. It is easier to capture a sizable amount of the value delivered with a new offering because prices almost always go down over time. We say almost because absolutes are dangerous but if you look out over a long enough time period, it's hard to find something that doesn't become cheaper in relative currency.

Sustainable Pricing

Sustainability is an especially tricky part of pricing. If you set your price too high, it could encourage potential buyers to expand their search for alternatives. Setting a high price shines a big light on other options available in the market. This could drive customers to attempt to develop in-house alternatives, or competitors to develop cheaper ways to solve all or part of the problem you solve.

The bottom line is that you need to understand how sustainable and defensible your differentiation is over time. There are great consumer product examples on this.

On one hand, we have a pharmaceutical company developing a new drug to treat or cure disease. (This is not a philosophical or ethical debate about how much the company *should* charge for the drug, but a discussion of economic reality.) Besides potentially spending billions of dollars on research and development, the company has a limited amount of time before a generic version of the drug can be made by competitors.

Once generic versions hit the market, the price usually drops by up to 85%. Thus, during the time that the drug is under patent, the price they charge is based on the next best alternative at the time. Because this alternative is often a very expensive surgery or worse, the price they can charge can be very high.

Let's assume the alternative is a surgical or medical procedure that costs $20,000, and the patent protects the drug for eight years. The payer should be willing to pay up to $200 per month for the drug to avoid the procedure. Once the patent expires, the next best alternative is a generic drug that may cost only 15% to 20% of the original price. This means the price of the original drug would need to drop to roughly $40 to be competitive. The pharmaceutical company has an eight-year run at five times their final price. In this case, the profit-optimizing price is very close to the maximum price.

At the other end of the spectrum, say you have an offering that can easily be copied within six months. The company has two choices: charge a price that captures significant value and then lower prices when competitors enter and hope you don't lose good will with customers, or charge a lower price to start with and grow profits by gaining market share.

Walmart provides a consumer example of this latter approach. During the 1990s, Walmart drove hundreds of millions of dollars in cost saving from its suppliers. But rather than pocketing the extra margin, they passed nearly all of it along to their customers. They were rewarded with tremendous growth, opening an average of 250 stores per year in the US for the decade.

Cost Structure

Your customer's cost structure is another consideration in establishing value pricing. If the cost of your offering is a small percentage of their overall cost, you can likely price to capture more of the value created. However, if your offering is a major portion of their expenditures, they will be more sensitive to your price. You'll need to share much more of the value created to get the customer to move.

Market Size and Share

Market size, market share, and the impact on current customers are important considerations when determining value pricing. Ask yourself these questions to better understand your environment and the ramifications of your decisions.

- Is there a large part of the market that could be addressed at a lower price?

- Are there segments of the potential market where the cost of solving the problem is too great to be affordable, even if it creates significant value?

- Could you penetrate untapped market segments with a scaled down version of your offering at a lower price?

- Would you generate greater net profit by addressing these untapped markets or by addressing the current identified market?

Then ask yourself if there are segments of customers that are more or less price sensitive within the current identified market. Remember, price sensitivity is the observed symptom, but the root cause is something about the differences in customer value.

Those observed differences in sensitivity may be due to perceived value, their sophistication and ability to realize and measure value, or their availability of investment dollars. What's the size of each of those segments? Can you price differentiate between them? Will a higher price with a lower market share deliver more earnings than a lower price with a higher market share?

Finally, you need to consider the impact your pricing will have on customers that are already buying products or services from you. Even if you deliver high value, a high price that captures a significant portion of that value could cause those customers to stop buying other things from you. If that's likely the case, be sure to factor in the negative earnings impact from the loss of those other sales.

The goal of this exercise is to be very honest about where the market is today, and how all of these factors could change over time. Then build your best estimates of what's likely to happen, based on various pricing decisions. This allows you to choose the price that will maximize the long-term returns your business will receive from your offering, based on all the information you know today.

Unless you have a crystal ball, you will never have perfect information about the future. This thought experiment will at least provide enough insight to make an informed decision.

Here is a table that helps to evaluate each of these factors and how they should impact your price:

SITUATION	PRICE TO SHARE MORE VALUE	PRICE TO KEEP MORE VALUE
Next best alternative's ability to lower price	High	Low
Ability of competitors to duplicate offering	High	Low
Time for competitors to duplicate offering	Short	Long
Percentage of customer's cost structure	High	Low
Total market elasticity	High	Low

Sample Value Pricing: Integrated Offering

Imagine you sell both fire detection and video monitoring solutions to a variety of industries. You have been working on a solution for marine applications where a typical ocean-going cargo ship could eliminate one crew member by integrating its fire and video systems. The annual cost of a crew member aboard a ship is about $500,000 including insurance, room and board, and benefits. The next best alternative would be to have a systems integrator develop a custom software solution which would cost $180,000 per ship and take six months to complete.

With all of that in mind, the incremental value and maximum price can be calculated as follows:

$$\text{Value} = V - V_{nba} = \$500,000 - \$250,000 = \$250,000$$

$$P_{max} = P_{nba} + \text{Value} = \$180,000 + \$250,000 = \$430,000$$

Note that the $250,000 in incremental value is a one-time savings due to fielding the system six months faster than a bespoke system.

How would you think about pricing this offering? Let's walk through the various elements that will guide us towards how we can price this offering.

Let's start with the impact on the customer. This is a direct cost reduction since it allows them to reduce one full headcount from the ship and as such, customers are likely to be willing to share more of the savings. The magnitude of the savings being $500,000 per year makes it interesting, but not their biggest expense.

Also, since this is an offering that customers have never seen before, there is no underlying expectation of what it should cost, except relative to how much savings they will receive. These are all good things and none of them would preclude you from capturing upwards of 50% of the value created.

Next, let's look at the competition, or the next best alternative. The competition is not likely to lower their prices since they make money on integration labor, which is good. But this is relatively easy to copy in a relatively short period of time. Pricing too high would motivate customers to find an integrator to deliver a similar solution for less money. And, once a competitor delivers the solution to one ship, they could likely deliver the solution in less time on the next ship, especially for a large fleet of similar ships. Sharing more of the value would accelerate penetration and could help to keep competition out of the market.

This one factor will significantly impact your ability to capture a significant portion of the value. In order to keep customers from finding an alternative, thus creating a competitor, you will likely need to share a larger percentage of the relative value created. You probably would need to price the offering much closer to the alternative of $180,000, even though the maximum theoretical price is $430,000.

Summary

The next time someone tells you that they are going to market with a skimming price strategy at a 10% premium, you now have the tools to ask some pointed questions to validate their decision.

- How is your competition likely to respond to that price?

- How quickly can alternative solutions be developed to undermine your value?

- Why 10% and not 50% or even 200%?

If they can't answer these questions, challenge their assumptions and dig deeper. Don't accept answers like, "Our brand commands a 10% premium" or worse, as Nigel from *Spinal Tap* says, "Ours goes to eleven."

Pricing is one of the most critical factors in determining the success of an offering. Underprice and you won't have the margins to continue investing in the offering and grow your market. Overprice and you won't sell much, or you will encourage competitors to enter the market and push you out over time.

Although pricing is hard work, it is one of the most important and rewarding parts of business leadership. Don't leave it to chance by arbitrarily choosing a strategy without first seeking to find the optimal price. And remember, the concept of optimal is meaningless unless it is grounded in a firm understanding of customer value.

9

Business Model

What is a business model? Like most terms that are overused, business model means different things to different people. For example, internet companies may refer to a "per click business model" when this is actually just an approach to pricing.

Although pricing is part of a business model, to us, the business model means so much more.

A Working Definition

A business model is the formula through which a business makes money. It must incorporate what you sell (offering) to whom (target segments) in a unique way (differentiation) to deliver how much customer value (value proposition) and capture a portion of that value (pricing model) enabled by what critical things (resources).

The goal of Grassroots Strategy is to build a better business using a coherent business model, not produce pretty PowerPoint presentations that cover an empty slogan. In addition to everything we've defined so far, a good strategy has to answer one more question: "What changes Monday morning?"

At a minimum, your business model must be able to make, sell, and deliver your value proposition and provide a mechanism through which customers will pay. As one of our clients says, "The business model is your recipe for making money." And like any good recipe, it includes all the ingredients you need together with guidance on how you process them.

Your business model includes the critical elements of how you communicate and deliver your value proposition, including:

- The target segments you will serve

- Your differentiated value for each target segment

- How you will communicate to and interact with customers (go to market plan)

- How you will manufacture and deliver your offering

- Your pricing approach (the unit that you are pricing and the charging mechanism)

- How you will measure success

And it must answer one absolutely critical internal question: what ongoing mechanisms will you invest in to make your offering more valuable over time? For example, how will you build scale, level, and focus of R&D spending? How will you derive learnings from customer service data?

Fixed or Flexible?

We are discussing this concept now, in part, as a caution to not cast your current business model in stone. By the way, if your company has been around for a while, you already have a business model, whether or not you call it that or recognize it as such. Now is a good time to revisit it.

Too many B2B companies assume that since they've always done things a certain way, they shouldn't change what is working. Examples including getting paid for shipping tanker cars of chemicals or putting parts in boxes and selling them through a distributor. It doesn't have to be that way, and maybe it really shouldn't be that way. If there is a better way to serve customers someone will eventually figure it out, and it's that much better if it is you.

Alternative ways of making money have been around for a long time in the B2B world. In the automotive and aerospace industries, breakeven pricing is often given to original equipment manufacturer (OEM) customers in order to make money in the aftermarket. Or, a product is deeply discounted to make money on servicing it. Office copiers used to work this way, as did cell phones in the consumer world, at least until the introduction of the iPhone.

And while we may take it for granted now, GE's famous "power by the hour" method of selling jet engines was a real game changer at the time. It eliminated the acquisition price of the engine and merged everything into a single, simple, and entirely variable cost per engine hour fee that included ongoing costs for inspection, maintenance, and financing.

If you are considering new ways to add value for your customers, it's a great time to rethink your business model. Many winning business models developed innovative mechanisms for delivering value and getting paid. Some get paid per unit of your customer's output, or a charge for a service that has historically been free. Others might sell access to technical data as an annual subscription.

Many payment mechanisms are enabled by the rapidly connected and digitized world and the growth of the Internet of Things. The decreasing cost of computer memory and processing speed make many more options possible. But business model innovation has been taking place long before there was an internet.

Case Study: Industrial Gas Suppliers

A significant business model change occurred in the industrial gas business about 30 years ago. Companies in this business deliver various gases to industrial plants for use in manufacturing processes.

Except for some highly specialized applications where high levels of purity are needed, the products themselves are nearly always commodities. Because the products are chemically identical to each other regardless of which company delivers them, the differentiation must be in the service.

With multiple equivalent sources of supply, most customers exhibited a high degree of price sensitivity. But over time, the industrial gas companies realized that the price they were charging for the gas itself was but a fraction of the total acquisition and administrative cost that their customers incurred. Their customers had to:

- Track their **inventory** of gases. This is not an easy task since a full cylinder looks the same as an empty one and a cylinder of oxygen looks the same as a cylinder of hydrogen if the label comes off.

- Determine **replenishment** cycles that defined how frequently to reorder, in what quantity, and sometimes in what size of cylinder.

- Manage the **logistics** of unloading, transporting, and connecting new cylinders and recharging/recycling old ones.

- Worry about the **safety** and liability of storing and handling these gases, some of which are poisonous and/or explosive, which was usually not their core competency.

In retrospect, the solution seems obvious: a turnkey system that simplifies acquiring and replenishing gas for industrial manufacturing. The gas companies would install secure onsite areas for gas storage, and even gas production in many cases, so that no customer employee would have to enter. They would remotely monitor gas usage and charge only for actual consumption. And they would use this information to automatically trigger replenishment, sending and installing replacement gas cylinders before the old ones ran out.

As you can imagine, they were able to charge a premium for these services because they dramatically lowered the risk and hassle of buying and handling industrial gases. Moreover, customer satisfaction went way up when this headache was eliminated.

Surprisingly, the logistics cost of servicing these customers went down. By monitoring usage, the gas companies were able to detect patterns and design predictable, efficient delivery routes and make more informed decisions about when and how to use on-site production. This was much more efficient than constantly disrupting logistics to fill emergency orders from customers who didn't realize they were low on a specific gas until it actually ran out.

This example highlights the power of a business model in creating value and changing the game in terms of how you get paid. It's a great story, but it is missing one important piece.

No matter how ground-breaking at the time, the services described were relatively easy to copy. So in short order, the next best alternative was once again a competing gas company using the new business model to drive down prices and limit the ability to capture value.

That is why we are so insistent that a business model has to be more than just a clever pricing scheme.

Building a Flywheel-Based Business Model

We have mentioned the flywheel business model in previous chapters, so now let's dig into what we mean.

To improve differentiation over time and ultimately achieve sustainability, a good business model must do more than support your strategy. It must build a foundation that improves scale or knowledge in order to continuously improve your offering over time and provide more value than copycats can deliver.

Said differently, a good business model looks at what are you doing with today's customers that makes you better, smarter or cheaper in serving tomorrow's customers. Companies that get this right develop flywheel-based business models.

Business Model "Flywheel"

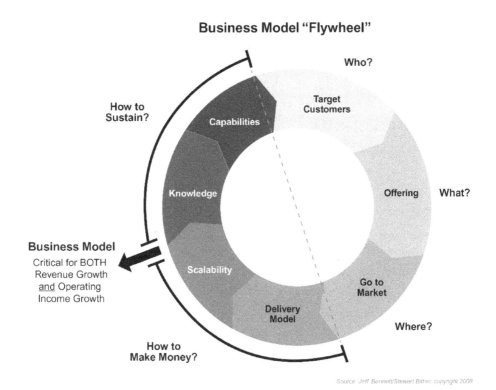

Source: Jeff Bennett/Stewart Bither, copyright 2008

The concept is pretty straightforward. If your delivery model for serving current customers is building some combination of scale, knowledge, and capability that improves with time, then you are building a flywheel business. If you are customizing everything for each customer and not following up to see why some customers are more satisfied than others, then you are not. This is not to say that non-flywheel businesses are necessarily bad. Sometimes they can produce very high margins, but they are also highly susceptible to competition and are not scalable.

As an extreme example, brain surgery is an expertise-driven business with thankfully, very high barriers to entry. But brain surgery is not a flywheel business. The surgeon's incredible knowledge and skill are entirely in his head and when he stops doing surgeries, he stops getting paid. It's a very nice living, but it is not scalable. The surgeon gets paid per surgery at the same rate whether he performs 100 or 1,000 surgeries in a year.

Contrast this with someone who invents a new procedure for making brain surgery safer. If the process can be protected as intellectual property, it can be licensed. And if the inventor collects a fee each time the process is used, it is scalable. Further, if the inventor gathers data on specific applications and fine tunes the procedure over time (making it easier to train someone, for example), its advantages are sustainable, even as copies of the original concept come to market.

Sustainability has long been the holy grail of business strategy. In classic strategy, the only way to achieve sustainable differentiation is with a cost advantage based on unique assets: owning all the best lithium mines, for example, or driving down costs by riding the experience curve.

The business model gives us another alternative. A flywheel business can be sustainable for decades, even with no patented intellectual property. The key is the behind-the-scenes capability that enables the business to improve with each iteration.

Case Study: Amazon

A great example of this is Amazon. Amazon is a massive company that does many things well. But if we look at their core business of selling things online (originally books, but now almost anything), how do they differentiate?

Nearly everything Amazon sells is available somewhere else on the web at exactly the same price. Yes, Amazon is easy to use, but so are other websites. And, Amazon has mastered running a massive and efficient logistics network, yet they lose money on shipping.

They didn't invent the logistics either. Walmart had a world class logistics network before Amazon even existed. So, what is their secret?

It is the one capability that we take for granted that is the most difficult to copy. Amazon calls it their "recommendation engine," the behind-the-scenes algorithms that enable them to suggest related items you might also like (Mangalindan, 2012).

What makes this capability virtually impossible to copy is the data behind it. Amazon has a complete record of everything you ever bought from them and since at least 2007, they have captured what you looked at but did not buy. As a result, their recommendations are systematically better than anyone else's.

How good? Well, Amazon does not release a number, but some analysts estimate that recommendations generate as much as 35% of their sales (Natanson, 2017). What this means is you could invest billions of dollars to copy everything else about Amazon but because you can't replicate this capability, you will likely never achieve more than 65% of their revenue.

Now the logic of Amazon Prime begins to make sense. Although Amazon loses money on free shipping (Bishop, 2017), they acquire massive amounts of data to help them make more and better recommendations. This makes them the easy choice for everything you buy online and in their aspirations, everything you buy, period. Bought these gardening tools? How about this book on gardening, some seeds, and plant food? The recommendations are endless.

As an aside, do not dismiss Amazon as a B2C example. They are aggressively penetrating B2B markets with products and increasingly, with services. Several of our clients who never considered having an e-commerce strategy have been surprised to find their products on Amazon's website. How did they get there?

Their distributors found it to be an effective channel for reaching incremental customers and/or selling excess inventory.

Even if you have not yet experienced this, you have probably noticed the "Amazonification" of B2B. As your customers get used to Amazon's service in their personal lives, they increasingly expect the same level and type of service with their professional purchases. At the very least, you should be thinking about providing your customers with services like multiple and easy search methods (by application *and* part number, for example), product reviews, real-time inventory, transparent terms, and accurate ship dates.

Characteristics of a Flywheel Business Model

Based on our ongoing experience studying diverse flywheel business models, we have compiled a list of common characteristics. Some of these are counter-intuitive, so we want to share the characteristics and a consumer example that brings them to life.

Nearly all the flywheel businesses that we studied:

1. Did not invent the product or category

2. Questioned conventional wisdom about their industry

3. Discovered an overlooked or underserved segment

4. Clearly understood the needs of that segment

5. Translated those needs into the one or two things they had to do better than anyone else, every day

6. Aligned their entire organization around consistently delivering on those one or two things

Let's begin with Southwest Airlines to illustrate how these characteristics work.

Case Study: Southwest Airlines

Every year since 1973, just two years after its inaugural flight, Southwest Airlines has been profitable (Schleckser, 2018). Contrast that with the airline industry as a whole, which lost more money between 1990 and 1994 than it had made in total since 1930.

Southwest was clearly not the first airline in the US; nor were they the first discount carrier. But they distinguished themselves by questioning conventional wisdom.

When Southwest was founded, every other airline made its money on business travelers, who were considered the least price-sensitive customers. These airlines used increasingly complex pricing requirements (advance purchase, Saturday night stay, etc.) to ensure that business travelers paid more, while they filled planes with vacation and leisure travelers at lower fares.

Southwest did exactly the opposite by focusing on price-sensitive vacation and leisure travelers. Rather than employ complex and dynamic pricing algorithms, they charged low, flat fares every day.

The truth is more complicated, according to *NUTS!*, the popular book about Southwest Airlines' cofounders, Herb Kelleher and Rollin King, and the company's unique approach to business success (Frieberg & Frieberg, 1996). According to the book, King's banker, John Parker, had "…complained to King that it was inconvenient and expensive to travel between Houston, Dallas, and San Antonio and suggested starting an intrastate airline."

At the time, the oil industry had many independent consultants and operators who paid their own expenses. Their travel alternatives were either taking the bus for about $30 or flying with Braniff, one of the only carriers covering all three markets, for $600 to $900 round trip.

Southwest certainly addressed this unmet business need when it launched, but it quickly realized that the larger market segment was price-sensitive vacation and leisure travelers. Many of these travelers wanted to fly, but rarely did so primarily because of the price.

So, what were the travel options for this price-sensitive segment before Southwest Airlines came along?

- Fly on a very expensive full-service airline

- Drive, which is time-consuming and assumes they own a reliable car

- Take a lengthy bus ride, stopping in every small town and losing control of who sits in the next seat

- Take a passenger train, if they are lucky enough to live in one of the few US locations with reasonable service, or any service at all

- Not travel at all

It's pretty clear that none of these options compare to the convenience of a low-cost airline flight.

Now here's the critical part. As Southwest focused on the needs of the vacation and leisure segment, they translated those needs into two priorities that must be met every day. The first is essential: if you offer everyday low fares, you had better have low costs. There's no way around it.

The second and less obvious priority addresses the needs of the inexperienced travelers that make up their core market. Most took only one or two trips a year and, especially in the 1970s, many had never been on a plane before. Unlike full-fare carriers that cater to frequent flyers and experienced travelers, Southwest had to go above and beyond to be not just hassle free, but genuinely easy to use at every step in the traveling process. This started with buying a ticket and ended with claiming their luggage.

Southwest chose the word "fun" to describe the experience they aspired to deliver to every passenger. Fun goes beyond just having a pleasant experience. It gives passengers something to talk about when they get to their destination. And since their customers' next best alternative was often not to fly at all, over-delivering on fun gave passengers a reason to come back. *(You know, I wasn't planning on going to cousin Shirley's wedding in Oklahoma City this summer, but I had such a great time on Southwest and the fares are so cheap, I think I'll go!)*

Now we get to the heart of what makes a flywheel business so hard to copy. Because Southwest is laser focused on low cost and fun as their two overarching priorities, they built systems, policies, and procedures that differ from every other airline. And it's not just one or two things that are different. There are perhaps thousands of differences that affect everything Southwest does, every day, and result in a customer experience that no other airline can match.

Remember Delta's "Song," United's "TED," and the horribly named "Continental Light" before Continental merged with United? All claimed to be discount carriers patterned after Southwest, and all of them failed. Why? Because they copied the most obvious things about Southwest (low fares, no frills) but couldn't come close to copying the hundreds of operational nuances and differences that make Southwest successful.

For Southwest's target customers, their experiences with these alternate carriers was still slightly more expensive and not nearly as good service as Southwest. Worse yet, by eliminating valuable amenities such as pre-boarding and first-class upgrades, the airlines dramatically worsened the experience for their most profitable segment, frequent business travelers. It's no wonder they failed!

Let's look deeper at some of Southwest's operational differences. A big one is that Southwest flies just one type of plane, the Boeing 737. The cost implications from this one thing are huge! They only need one set of spare parts and one set of operating, crew, and maintenance manuals. And if a plane is grounded for unplanned maintenance, they can swap it with any other plane in their fleet.

Could a legacy carrier copy this aspect? They could, but they would have to give up any route that could not be serviced by a 737. This might be as much as half of their route map and worse, it would eliminate all long-haul international flights where many airlines make most of their money.

Now consider the impact of a single-plane fleet on their broader business processes. When Southwest decides to add a new city pair to its route structure, they already know what type of plane they will fly. The cost and management time associated with making this decision is zero. This is so fundamental to their business model that it is safe to assume that if Southwest ever does add a second type of plane to their fleet, it will require Board of Directors approval.

In contrast, when legacy carriers add a new city pair, they convene a network analysis group comprised of very smart people with advanced degrees in mathematics, statistics, and network analysis. This group builds models based on projected passenger loads and calculates the optimal plane to fly that route.

But what is the outcome of all this work? By using the optimal plane on each route, their fleet ends up with many different aircraft and even more different plane configurations. If you're reading this on a plane, pull the airline's magazine out of the seat pocket in front of you and flip to the page that talks about their fleet.

Consider the cost of parts and maintenance manuals for these aircraft, which can have a dozen different engine models manufactured by four different companies. This is anything but low cost. And how about that fun travel experience promised by Southwest? Have you ever had to stand in line with 200 people at O'Hare because there has been an "equipment" change" and everyone needs a new seat assignment? Definitely not fun.

Prerequisites for a Flywheel

Not every business can become a flywheel. The examples cited in this chapter also benefit from focusing on a single market and in some cases, having a visionary founder who continued to pursue a vision that was somewhat insulated from short term financial returns.

An extreme case is Amazon, where it took four years to show the first profitable quarter, six years to show two consecutive profitable quarters, and over 12 years to show positive cumulative earnings following its IPO in July of 1997. The business model is now cranking out profits and from July 2003 and the end of 2017, Amazon made a profit in all but six quarters. It took 14 years of cumulative profit to equal Amazon's profit in the fourth quarter of 2018 (Griswold & Karaian, 2018).

Flywheel businesses have other characteristics in common as well, some of which apply even if you are changing a business model within a large company.

1. They create a **step change in value**. Although incremental changes may create "stickiness" with current customers, they are not enough to create a flywheel. Funding the investments to build a flywheel requires more than a slight improvement in customer satisfaction. It requires a change in value that is viscerally different than competing alternatives.

2. They find a **target segment** from whom they can learn. This is closely related to the first criteria, as customers will likely forgive you for not quite getting it right if you create a big jump in value.

3. They create opportunities to **build scale or knowledge** differently than traditional competitors.

4. They have **line of sight** to at least the next revolution of the flywheel.

We will now illustrate these characteristics of a flywheel company using Walmart as an example.

Case Study: Walmart

Walmart created a significant increase in value for their target customers. Remember that Walmart was far from the first discount mass merchant. Kmart beat them to market by ten years. But Walmart chose a different target segment, trading areas that Kmart had rejected as too small to sustain a store. These small towns had precious few alternatives until Walmart began opening stores.

The alternatives at the time were mostly:

- Overpriced "main street" retailers with a limited selection. Customers could find a shirt in their size or the color they wanted, but probably not both.

- Department stores like Sears, who had a broad selection but not necessarily low prices. Plus, you had to drive upwards of 30 miles to get there. Sears in particular had built their merchandising strategy on a high/low model with artificially inflated prices and periodic sales on most items.

In contrast to either of these options, Walmart was on the outskirts of their town, and had most everything they needed at prices lower than they had ever imagined. Now that's a step change in value!

Because Walmart offered such tremendous value, the customers in its target segment could forgive them for having only eight of the ten items on their shopping list. They were willing to return because those eight items had the lowest prices to be found.

A flywheel only works if you are willing and able to test and learn. No matter how much you study a market, there are things you cannot learn until you actually launch, like Southwest discovering that the vacation/leisure traveler market was far larger than the independent business traveler market they initially targeted. Staying close to the business and making these adjustments while the stakes are still small is critical to the success of a flywheel. This is why having a target segment where you can learn is more important to getting the business model right than going directly for the largest existing segment that everyone else is targeting.

Before Walmart, large retailers like Sears and Kmart used scale almost exclusively for purchasing advantage. Their merchandising functions were charged with determining what to buy for each department and then negotiating the best prices and terms from suppliers. Individual store managers were then responsible almost exclusively for execution: sell what shows up, when it shows up.

Walmart was built on a different philosophy that allowed them to build scale differently than their competitors. Sam Walton personally ran its very first store for nearly 10 years. He inherently understood the hundreds of decisions made daily by the store managers and deeply appreciated that the information required to make those decisions was often local. Involving a distant headquarters not only slowed decisions, it increased the likelihood that they were wrong. In the old "brute force" version of scale, decisions were, at best, right on average, but wrong for nearly every individual store.

As Walmart grew, it used its scale to develop highly effective retail systems that arm store managers with data and build distribution networks capable of responding to locally driven demand. As anyone who has negotiated with Walmart knows, they still demand low prices, but they also understand total system cost. If buying smart means dumping inventory on stores where it won't sell, they won't do it.

This difference in using scale is subtle and perhaps best illustrated with a hypothetical example.

Both Walmart and Kmart carry small plastic swimming pools that are perfect for a toddler on a hot summer afternoon. Kmart would have used its scale to buy out a supplier's entire stock at a rock bottom price. And in the interest of efficiency, purchasing would have been done by their merchandising function, and the pools would probably be delivered to all stores at the same time.

But this is far from optimal. A huge percentage of these pools are sold during the first few hot days of the year, which varies widely by geography. Obviously, people in Miami would be buying pools a lot earlier in the year than those in Minneapolis! Additionally, store-to-store differences run deeper than that: suburban stores probably sell more pools than inner city stores where most people live in apartments without access to a backyard.

Alternatively, Walmart would have negotiated a price discount, but likely required the supplier to hold the inventory and respond quickly to individual store orders. This not only solves the timing by climate zone, but gives Walmart the ability to respond quickly to unexpected surges in demand, like an early heat wave in the Midwest.

And importantly, while Kmart's approach is dependent on a few smart merchandisers, Walmart's approach gets better with the addition of more data from more stores and improves over time as store managers learn from their mistakes and share their successes. In brief, Walmart has all the characteristics of a flywheel.

As an epilogue, Kmart did try to respond. They recognized store differences by creating merchandising groups by climate zone, size, urban/rural, etc. But no matter how many groups they created, it was still fundamentally a push system, ignoring the important information known only to the store manager. Kmart also tried, without success, copying Walmart's systems by hiring dozens of IT professionals away from Walmart. But, Kmart was stuck in the wrong business model and trying to copy Walmart's IT systems were simply not enough.

It is important to note that when a business creates a successful flywheel business model, it is rare for a competitor to beat them at their own game. A flywheel business will typically only be bested by a completely different flywheel business, usually one that starts with a different target segment.

Lastly, even when it started out, Walmart had line of sight to additional revolutions of the flywheel. Sam Walton did not set out to build the world's largest retailer. But, having traveled for years as a district manager for Ben Franklin stores, he understood the issues and options that consumers had in small towns. So he knew that any learnings that he had in the first couple stores would likely apply to many other locations.

Today, despite issues with its international expansion and an incomplete answer to the ongoing threat of online shopping, Walmart is still the world's largest private employer and retailer in terms of revenue (Fortune, 2017) and number of employees (Atlas, 2019). Its stock success has created three of the 13 richest people in the US as of 2018 (Forbes, 2018).

In contrast, Kmart has gone from a peak of almost 2,200 stores to just 365 stores in 2018, with more closing every quarter. Even after merging with Sears in 2005, Kmart is struggling for its very survival and Sears filed Chapter 11 Bankruptcy in 2018.

Linking Business Model to Pricing

An offering that creates significant value for its customers creates an opportunity to consider, and maybe even necessitates considering, alternative business models.

Suppose you traditionally charge $100 per unit of your offering and found a way to create $1,000 in additional value. It might be difficult to capture more than a small amount of the $1,000 created unless you change the business model and, in particular, what you are pricing. For instance, you may need to charge for an outcome or a share of the savings delivered instead of just charging for the offering.

For example, imagine you have developed a breakthrough heat recovery technology that turns wasted heat into electricity in an industrial setting. One application you are targeting is metal smelting operations where you currently don't sell much of anything. Your field trials show that this solution can reduce energy costs in a typical smelting plant by 20%, which equates to roughly $2 million per year. Your cost to produce and install the equipment is $800,000. There is also an ongoing maintenance cost of $100,000 per year. How would you think about pricing this offering?

If you assume the equipment will be used for at least five years, it will deliver a total of $10 million in savings, which depending on the customer's cost of capital is somewhere around $8 million in today's dollars. Can you charge anywhere near $8 million for the system? Certainly not.

Consider that the plant needs to see a return, likely with a payback period of no more than 18 months. This means they might buy the system outright for no more than about $2.85 million (1.5 years of energy savings minus the incremental maintenance cost over that time period). That is, of course, if they believe your stated benefits at 100%, which isn't likely. To get the plant to buy the system outright, you probably couldn't charge more than $2 to $2.5 million, which would mean you could capture a maximum of 30% of the total value using this traditional capital equipment business model.

There are, however, ways to change the nature of the discussion and the customer's view of the price you are charging. That could be as simple as installing the equipment for free and taking a share of the energy savings. But our experience is that over time, customers would likely tire of sending you checks and want to buy the equipment outright.

Let's turn this around. If you think about it, lowering energy costs is the problem being solved for the customer. What if you installed the equipment for free and charged the customer for the electricity produced at potentially 80% or 90% what they would pay the utility company? The beauty of this model is that they will always be better off and you would capture the majority of the value.

Whenever you can find ways to create appreciable value for your customer, you will have many more options in terms of how you serve them and get paid. Don't assume that the only way to do business is using your current or a traditional business model.

Summary

A well-functioning business model is essential to implementing a strategy. No matter how good a strategy sounds on paper, it must actually deliver on the value proposition to customers and provide a clear pricing model to capture value.

Importantly, being trapped in your current business model can constrain your strategic thinking. Even the best business models have a limited lifespan. Rather than rejecting ideas that don't fit your current business model, we recommend that you consider designing the right business model to implement your new strategy.

We believe that the role of the business model is more important than ever for B2B companies. As professional purchasing organizations rapidly turn many products and services into commodities, the business model itself can become a key differentiator. For companies like Amazon and Southwest, who have built flywheel business models, this differentiation can be sustainable for long periods of time.

Like much of what we have talked about, business model innovation is not easy. In fact, it can be extremely difficult, especially within an organization whose current business model is successful. But like most of what we have talked about, the payoff for getting it right can be enormous, despite the difficulty. In some cases, it can result in decades of increasing profits.

The cost of getting it wrong can be significant as well. Too many companies learn the hard way that sticking with an outdated business model for too long can be fatal.

Before you declare your strategy finished, consider the potential impact on your business model:

- Is there a different way to deliver value?

- Is there a different way to get paid?

- Can you create scale and/or knowledge that's hard to replicate?

- What are you doing today that makes you better/smarter/more valuable for the customers of tomorrow?

The answers need not be dramatic. Lots of great incremental ideas fit within existing business models. But if you have three or four of the prerequisites for a flywheel business, don't set your sights too low. It could be the start of a once-in-a-lifetime business journey.

10

Testing Hypotheses for Market Insight

A senior executive at a customer of ours always gives project teams this charge after they finish a Grassroots Strategy session:

> *First, good work, but you've been working in a conference room with no windows and no customers. Although you may have made some good assumptions, you need to go test them with the market. Because despite all of your good work, the only thing we can guarantee at this point is that YOU ARE WRONG. We don't know if you are a little wrong or a lot wrong, but at least something in your hypotheses is wrong. It is now your job to figure out what is wrong and correct it before you go to market.*

When we introduced our Grassroots Strategy framework in Chapter 2 (Market-Back Framework), we discussed how easy it is to do the "strategy short-circuit" and jump from an idea directly to developing a go-to-market plan to launch the product.

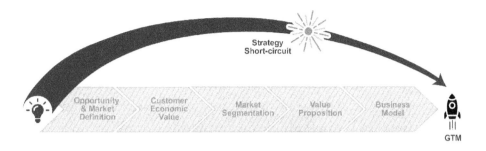

Throughout the subsequent chapters, we walked through the process of developing a strategy hypothesis. We say hypothesis because at this point, it hasn't been tested to verify its assumptions. This is where the second strategy short-circuit comes into play. It's not enough to have a hypothesis that sounds good. Testing is essential to sort out strategies that are plausible from those that are most likely to succeed.

The amount of testing needed greatly depends on the size of the bet you're making. If you can make small investments and test the concepts in small increments, then by all means, do that. However, if you need to invest millions of dollars in R&D for a product launch, then it becomes more important to test your hypothesis before making the investment.

B2C companies often have large market research budgets and can do massive amounts of customer testing using well known data, research providers, and techniques. B2B companies tend to have both smaller budgets and fewer customers. In this chapter, we will emphasize not only the importance of using hypotheses to test ideas in a B2B environment, but also the use of VoC (Voice of the Customer) as a critical, and often poorly implemented, technique for testing hypotheses.

Why Companies Avoid Testing

There are many reasons companies don't spend the time and money to test their hypotheses before going to market. First and foremost is that sometimes it can work. If you have a really good idea, sometimes it's better to move fast with a partially baked solution than to slow down and delay its launch. The problem is that this will fail more often than it succeeds.

We all hear about the success stories, but no one talks about the large number of failures for every single success.

Another and perhaps more prevalent reason to short-circuit the process is that it's both hard work and not fun to slow down and do the research. It is much more fun to come up with an idea and excitedly develop and promote a go-to-market plan than it is to do tedious research.

When it comes to launching a new offering, we have all seen these common approaches that usually end in failure.

- **Predetermining the Plan.** Have you ever been in a situation where a leader says something like, "I know our growth is going to come from China, so go figure out how we can grow in China?" This is a version of the short circuit – jumping straight to the more comfortable "how" questions without really understanding the "why."

  This approach is sometimes tacitly rewarded, as organizations mistake the level of detail in a plan for the quality of the logic, but it is dangerous. It is very easy to assemble data that support a foregone conclusion, even if it is incorrect.

- **Accepting Conventional Wisdom.** Conventional wisdom is almost always eventually wrong. Consider Apple's launch of the iPhone. At the time, conventional wisdom said no one would pay for a mobile phone because it came free as part of the mobile service. That was true until Apple launched a significantly better phone for which people were willing to pay $700.

- **Analysis Paralysis.** In business, it is appropriate to question the validity of a decision and feel discomfort launching a new product without sufficient data and underlying details. But too often, asking for more information becomes a reflexive response (or a way to cover someone's backside) and organizations forget that their job is to make a "good enough" decision and move on. In consulting, this is often referred to as "boiling the ocean."

  Boiling the ocean may be a very effective way to fish, but it is not very efficient. And if you were actually able to do it (which we don't advise), you would kill all of the fish including a whole lot that you don't want. Think back to Chapter 3 (Opportunity and Market Definition). You can stop your analysis when both ends of your projected range of outcomes lead you to the same decision.

- **Planning without Thinking.** This is way too common with inexperienced business professionals. "But it worked in the spreadsheet! We raised prices by 10% and our profit went up by 50%!" The problem is that the spreadsheet didn't take into account the potential lost customers when the new price was higher than the relative value created. As a result, their volumes and profitability went down when they raised prices.

> Projects don't fail because no one could figure out how to make the numbers look attractive in a spreadsheet – projects fail because the assumptions behind the numbers are insufficiently tested or worse, not even articulated.

So, how do you avoid these traps? Easy. You start with a set of hypotheses that can be tested. Well, maybe it's not that easy.

These traps can be hard to avoid because of something called confirmation bias. This is the tendency to remember and/or give more weight to information that supports your existing beliefs. Studies have repeatedly demonstrated the prevalence of this bias, even among highly educated people (Haidt, 2013).

For example, people will find more faults in a report if it contradicts their position on an important issue, such as a study on the effectiveness of capital punishment. Recent work in neuroscience suggests that this bias is actually hard-wired. Information that confirms a bias is more pleasing and it affects the emotional centers in the brain before it even processes the information into a conscious understanding!

Overcoming this bias is difficult, but not impossible. Two best practices to overcome bias are to have people with competing hypotheses on the team, and to consciously look for disconfirming evidence by asking, "If we are wrong, what are we likely to see?" Admitting you are wrong is never easy, but it is better to do it before you have spent millions of dollars to launch a failed product. On the bright side, we have found that almost every rejected hypothesis leads to a new idea or opportunity. When you invest in understanding your market, you almost always learn something.

Using and Testing Hypotheses

We won't spend much time discussing the scientific method we all learned in middle school science, but we will reference some key points and talk about how the scientific method works in marketing as well.

As a quick refresher, let's start with a diagram showing the scientific method and how it works.

- Start with a hypothesis that is based on observations of how things work.

- Develop a set of predictions of what you expect to observe based on a set of tests.

- Test those predictions. If, over time, your predictions are consistent

Source: UC- Riverside, Dept. of Physics. www.physics.ucr.edu

with the outcomes of your tests, you can be more confident in your hypothesis, at which time it becomes a theory.

It is key to remember that in using the scientific method, you are actually trying to prove your hypothesis wrong, not prove it right. It is far easier to assemble the data to support your conclusion than it is to design and build tests that prove your hypothesis wrong.

If you can't disprove your hypothesis, you can be reasonably confident (but never absolutely sure) that it is correct. On the other hand, if your observations do not fit your hypothesis, then you either refine the hypothesis to reflect the new learnings or reject it outright.

A few additional thoughts on testing your hypothesis.

- **You can't prove a negative.** Build your hypothesis around stating a positive. Then try to prove it false. For example, try proving that Bigfoot does not exist to a believer. No matter how much evidence you provide, they will always come up with an answer as to why you didn't prove his nonexistence.

    Even if you cut down all the trees in the Pacific Northwest and don't find Bigfoot, you still haven't proven that Bigfoot does not exist. What would a true believer say? That Bigfoot is smart and he knew you were coming, so he went north into Canada. You can build a case that something is likely to be true with a body of evidence, but you can never prove that something is false.

- **Try a counter-intuitive hypothesis.** If everyone believes that X is true, why not come up with another explanation for why things work the way they do? Think back to our Walmart example of conventional wisdom saying that small towns wouldn't support a major retailer. Or perhaps the air travel example where airlines made all their money on long-haul business travelers until Southwest Airlines came along.

- **It's okay to have competing hypotheses.** This can be very important for team dynamics. If the entire team doesn't agree on a single hypothesis, then develop hypotheses for each of the alternative ideas and develop plans to test each of them. Don't argue about what you believe to be true. Develop tests to determine what is actually true.

An example from early in one of our consulting careers helps make this point. I was working with a client in the automotive aftermarket who had just completed a market segmentation. I was highly suspicious of the client's demographic-based approach, especially because nearly every time it was applied, one-third of consumers ended up in each of the three segments – exactly the result you would expect if it was random.

The client had spent a lot of money on the study and didn't like this hypothesis, but rather than argue, we agreed on a test. If I was right and the results were random noise, then we wouldn't expect to see market-share differences across the segments. We were able to cross-reference the segmentation study with other research and found that their market share varied wildly across the segments, from a low of 6% to a high of over 30%. As this was definitely not random, I was sheepishly forced to reject my hypothesis. Fortunately, it was a very understanding client and we have remained friends.

Remember, when you uncover facts that are inconsistent with your hypothesis, modify the hypothesis rather than sweep those facts under the rug. Humility and flexibility are key to making this approach work.

Issue Diagram

An issue diagram is a helpful tool for organizing your hypotheses and the tests that need to be performed to analyze and test them. Here is a template for an issue diagram:

Issue	Hypotheses	Key Questions (Tests)	Analysis	Data
▸	▸		▸	

You begin by listing the core business issues you are trying to solve, followed by the hypotheses for addressing each of those business issues. Then you identify a set of questions whose answers will test your hypotheses. Think of the questions in terms of what must be true for this hypothesis to be valid.

In the next column, define a set of analyses to be performed to test the hypothesis. By entering the name and due date in the last column, you have completed a work plan that you know will address your business issues.

Here are some considerations on designing analyses to test hypotheses. The best way to test a hypothesis is often indirectly. For example, we had a client who made protective footwear for a variety of dangerous environments. They wanted to figure out if they could charge a premium for a more durable work boot for firefighters.

Directly testing this hypothesis would likely not work. If you simply ask customers if they would pay more for a more durable boot, the reflexive answer might be "no" to discourage you from raising prices. Conversely, the answer might be a thoughtless "yes." After all, you will be spending your development dollars, not theirs, to develop the new boot, and purchasing can always negotiate the price down later.

What the client did was talk to customers about the specifying and buying process. They discovered that most fire departments budget to buy new boots for all their firefighters every three years. They run a public tender process and are required to buy from the lowest bid that meets industry standards. In other words, the boots only need to last three years, making it difficult to get paid for additional durability. More importantly, they know the "why" behind this finding and can change their response if the situation or standards changes in the future.

Case Study: Paint Ingredient

Let's illustrate how an issue diagram works to build confidence.

This project was for a client that manufactures a paint ingredient. Like acrylic, this ingredient is used as a binder in paint. Historically, it was only used in low-end paint sold mostly in Latin America. Every few years someone would ask sales, "Why aren't you selling more of our product into paint applications? We are we selling it in Latin America, but nowhere else." And, thinking it was a sales targeting problem, they would set higher quotas in the rest of the world, but never achieved any noticeable change in sales.

They finally decided to evaluate their paint offering using the Grassroots Strategy process. As you can see in the issue diagram below, they defined the business issue around the need to compete with acrylic, the dominant binder for interior paint in most of the world. They speculated that there were two factors keeping them from selling more of their product in this application: the performance of their product vs. acrylic, and the branding of their product vs. acrylic.

Issue	Hypotheses	Key Questions (Tests)	Analysis	Data
▶ Current formulations struggle to compete with acrylic in higher end paints • Performance • Branding	▶ By expanding chemistry by using our ingredient, we can match acrylic performance at a lower total cost ▶ There is a segment of consumers who will pay a premium for "Eco-" benefits ▶ We can streamline processes for paint producers	• What properties are most important to define 'equivalent' performance? • What chemistries have already been investigated? • What premiums are consumers paying already? • What trends are reflected in purchase patterns? • Where are the issues in current paint manufacturing processes and where can we impact them?	• Survey of consumer research • VOC with paint marketing managers • Technical literature and patent search • Design of Experiments • Case studies of 'green' products in paint and related categories • Map the paint mfg. process and key differences across major producers	▶ ... ▶ ... ▶ ... ▶ ... ▶ ...

To address these issues, they created three hypotheses, five key questions to be answered, and an analysis plan that included primary research, secondary research, lab testing of their product vs. acrylic, and mapping the paint manufacturing process. Much of this insight into the customer's business would be obtained through VoC, which we will define more completely in just a few pages.

In the end, they were able to reject all three of the hypotheses, which is why we can talk about it so directly. Using an issue diagram allowed them to document that it was not a sales problem. There was just no value proposition for paint manufacturers to switch to their product, even when priced significantly below acrylic. Further, they documented their learnings so that unless something changed in the market or paint technology, they would not need to revisit this analysis every time someone raised the question.

Testing Hypotheses

As we mentioned earlier, it is very important to seek evidence that disproves your hypotheses instead of looking only for data that support them. It is both easy and enticing to gather data that support what you would like to be true. Although that may be gratifying in the short term, it does nothing to increase the chances that your strategy is sound.

As you saw in the paint additive example, there are different types of analyses and tests that may need to be performed to test your hypotheses. We believe that the most important information usually comes from VoC because it can lead to an in-depth understanding of customers and their needs. However, it is often helpful to start with secondary research to clarify what is already known.

This can include:

- Competitor analysis

- Reverse engineering

- Competitive teardowns

- Side-by-side testing

- Deep financial analysis of your customers' business or other market players

- Technical feasibility studies to determine what's really possible

Be sure to choose analyses that can disprove your hypotheses and then develop a test plan. And remember that secondary research is usually just the first step. Only one thing is certain in testing your hypotheses: it will involve talking to customers to gain market insight.

Market Insight

Market insight is an evolution of Voice of the Customer. Too often companies use the term VoC to describe something that is little more than a customer satisfaction survey of existing customers. Instead of just interviewing customers and asking how they feel about your current offerings, VoC and market insight focus on gaining deep insight into your customers' business.

Market insight is about becoming a "student of your customer." Over time, your goal is to understand their business and challenges better than they can articulate themselves. And, you are seeking to uncover unmet needs that enable you to address specific issues in their businesses. Even more importantly, you are looking for large enough groups of customers with similar needs (target segments) to constitute an interesting and successful business.

Taking a passive approach to VoC presents several problems. If you simply ask customers what they need, you'll usually find that they are not very good at articulating those needs. They may not even know they have a problem or that there is a way to solve the problem. And they certainly won't know the depth of your capabilities and therefore, how you could help them.

Case Study: Polymer

One of our clients had developed a high-strength polymer that could replace metal parts. In testing, they determined that their polymer had properties that allowed scrap from the molding process to be ground up and put back into the feed. Not only did this reduce the amount of material sent to a landfill, but it also reduced the amount of material they had to purchase. In contrast, other polymers in the market with equivalent performance attributes could not be recycled and all scrap had to be landfilled.

Before their Grassroots Strategy session, this customer was focused on finding customers that wanted to replace metal with polymer. After the session, they realized that they provided the most differential value to parts manufacturers already making plastic parts using competitive polymers. All they had to do was show potential customers how using their polymer could reduce their cost to produce the same parts with equivalent performance.

As part of their hypothesis testing, they began talking to parts manufacturers about their need to reduce scrap. There was one particular plant that they believed had high levels of scrap and was therefore in their target segment. But every time they asked the plant manager if they had a scrap problem, the frustrating answer was always a definitive "no."

Finally, they had the opportunity to tour the facility. As they were walking around, they noticed barrels of scrap everywhere. They asked the plant manager about the barrels and were told it was mold scrap from using a competitor's polymer. When challenged again about whether or not they had a scrap problem, the plant manager proudly replied, "I don't have a scrap problem. My budget for scrap is 12% and I am running at 10%." Little did he know that with our client's product they could be running less than 2% scrap!

The customer doesn't know what they don't know, and it is up to you to fill in the blanks. Observation can be as critical as the questions you ask.

To summarize, there are some significant differences between what we mean by market insight and traditional VoC.

MARKET INSIGHT SHOULD BE...	MARKET INSIGHT IS NOT...
A dialogue	A survey
Important at all levels of your customer base	Only talking to your current direct customers
About understanding the economics of your market	About understanding your customers' product feature ratings
Testing hypotheses	Confirming assumptions
An ongoing effort	A one-time event
About **quality** of insight	About **quantity** of insight
Finding un- or under-met needs	Asking for current performance requirements
About their business	About your products and features

Bottom line, market insight efforts should be measured in terms of what you learned and how it changed your business, not how many customers you talked to.

Tips from the Field

We won't insult you with basics like don't be rude and show up on time. Nor is it our intent here to give an exhaustive treatise on improving your interviewing skills. Instead, we'll focus on the most important considerations at this point in the hypothesis testing process.

Let's begin with the guideline that it's not about the quantity of data or the number of interviews. It's about gaining insight into your customers' business so you can help them make more money.

We are often asked how many customers you need to interview. Our answer is that you need to keep going until you can reasonably predict what the customer is going to say before you talk to them. In other words, stop when you are no longer surprised by their answers. That could be five interviews if you have a solid hypothesis and have properly segmented your market, or it could be dozens or even hundreds of interviews if that is not the case.

Hopefully, after every few interviews you are refining your hypotheses such that it won't take 100 interviews to get to a final answer. After almost every interview, you should go back and revisit your hypotheses and refine them based on what you learned.

Avoid the common problem of scripting the interview with too many questions. This sets the wrong tone because it begins to feel like an interrogation instead of a conversation. It is also less effective because if you plow through a long list of questions, you are less likely to slow down and ask "why" when something doesn't fit your hypothesis. In our experience, nearly all the important insights come from these follow-up questions.

Remember, the goal of these interviews is to test your hypotheses and look for other potential areas where you can help customers. You are looking for insights into the customer's business and how they make money. Until you talk to them and truly understand their issues, you are only guessing as to how you can help. Thus, you need to keep your topics open ended and at a high level. Ideally, you should be testing no more than three to five top level issues and asking enough questions to cover them adequately.

Here is a checklist we use to summarize your top issues and ensure you cover them completely in your interviews. Sometimes it helps to leave one or two columns blank for issues you didn't anticipate.

ISSUE				
Open	☐	☐	☐	☐
Clarify	☐	☐	☐	☐
Identify Root Causes	☐	☐	☐	☐
Quantify	☐	☐	☐	☐
Understanding Implications	☐	☐	☐	☐

Think of this like a bingo card where you check things off as you cover each area. Here's how it works:

- **Open.** Was this issue opened or brought up by either you or the customer?

- **Clarify.** Did you clarify that the customer means the same thing that you are thinking?

- **Identify Root Causes.** Did you ask the right "why" questions enough times to fully expose the underlying root cause?

- **Quantify.** Did you successfully quantify (in currency) the impact of this issue on their business?

- **Understand Implications.** And finally, did you get to the implications to their business and how important it is relative to the other issues?

One client tells her teams to start the interview like they are in a helicopter hovering at 10,000 feet, getting all the issues on the table before doing a deep dive into any one issue. This prevents you from focusing all your time on the issue that happens to be top-of-mind for the customer. Maybe it's something that just happened yesterday but if it only happens once every three years, it really isn't that big of a problem relative to other issues.

Try getting all the issues on the table while you are in helicopter mode at 10,000 feet. Then ask which issue they would focus on if they only had enough resources to solve one issue. Drill down into that issue before moving on to their next priority.

There are many ways this process can fail. Here are some reminders that can help ensure the success of testing your hypotheses.

- Talk to your customers outside of the sales cycle. You will rarely get honest input from a customer who thinks your questions are part of a sales negotiation.

- This is an ongoing process, not a one-time event.

- Don't ignore outliers. Dig deep to understand why they are different. You may have them in the wrong segment.

- If you can't quantify value, you can't price to value. Try to memorize the value equation and use it as a checklist.

- Don't assume that gathering a bunch of data is sufficient. If you didn't gain any insights, the data have no value.

- Ask the right questions to test your hypotheses and be open to accepting disconfirming evidence.

- Talk to multiple people, including up and down the value chain, to understand the market.

This section was intended to help you shift your perspective from satisfaction-focused VoC surveys to observing and interviewing customers to gain actionable insight. If you do this enough, you will discover that customers actually enjoy talking about their business, but rarely have the chance.

They can't always articulate what's important, so you will need to draw it out. Ask smart follow-up questions, especially those that start with "why." Think about quantification, customers may be more willing to share numbers than you think, especially if you build rapport and demonstrate knowledge about their business. Most importantly, this gets easier with practice, so just do it!

Summary

Don't build your go-to-market strategy in a room without windows or launch a new initiative before testing your hypotheses with customers. Although there is a slim chance you could be successful with that approach, it is more likely you will end up with an unsuccessful or moderately successful business, at best. Systematically test your hypotheses and avoid the strategy short-circuit!

11

Implications for Leaders

Hopefully we have made it clear by now that using the Grassroots Strategy process works. It is always better to test strategies or new products market-back than just going with your gut or "leaving it to the sales force to figure out." And because this approach is grounded in fundamental principles, you only have to learn it once. How you apply it may change as customers and technologies change, but the principles remain the same. We have seen this play out with clients who have brought this approach to new roles as their careers progress, sometimes across three or four companies.

What we have found is that this change in thinking boils down to a handful of principles that leaders can relatively easily keep in their heads. So let's review what we've said so far.

When customers buy a specific product or service, they do so to solve a problem or create a specific outcome. Make it a discipline to define your market as the problem you solve for the customer, not just the product you sell. This discipline also helps reveal alternative offerings and highlights potential threats.

Additionally, putting yourself in the customer's shoes frequently identifies adjacent unmet needs you may be able to solve, thus creating incremental sources of revenue.

Creating customer value is fundamental to your success. Remember the central tenet of business-to-business (B2B) marketing: if you can make more money for your customer, then they can pay you more. This requires differentiation, which is understanding (from your customers' perspective) what you do systematically better than your competitors.

Value is different than price and bears no relationship to cost. If you use cost-plus pricing, please stop. As discussed previously, cost-plus pricing has only two possible outcomes: you are pricing too low, or you are losing sales. There is no substitute for understanding your customers' economics and developing an objective view of how your differentiation creates value. There is also no substitute for being honest when and where you are not differentiated.

Different customers value different things, so segmenting markets based on differences in customer needs, and therefore value, can lead to breakthrough offerings and positions that are difficult to copy. On the flip side, accepting industry standard segmentations may simplify reporting, but it cannot provide insight and strategic advantage. Customers don't want "one size fits all," they want the one size that actually fits them. In B2B, this means having the right combination of features that solves their problems without being over-engineered with features they do not need.

Value propositions are the shorthand for articulating your market strategy for each target segment. A value proposition is not a sales pitch based on what you want the customer to believe. Rather, it is a simple, one-page template that captures descriptions of your target segment, your offering, your differentiation, what your offering is worth (value), and what you have to do to prove it. It's hard to believe how many companies still rush products to market without taking the time to document this foundation that should support any go-to-market plan.

Lastly, you need to understand and articulate your business model, which is your "recipe for making money." All businesses have a business model and all business models have a life cycle. Understanding how yours works is key to understanding both threats and opportunities. In addition, new sources of value sometimes enable and even necessitate breakthrough opportunities for new business models. The most sustainable business models create a flywheel: using today's business to learn and applying that knowledge to create even more value for customers in the future.

Organizational Alignment

Thus far, we have focused on using the market-back principles and process to test a specific growth strategy or product concept. But the real power of this approach is when it is adopted organization wide. A wave of energy is unleashed when key managers naturally ask each other the right questions and hold their strategies and plans to this higher standard.

Achieving this, however, is not easy. Adult learning is really about unlearning. It starts with acknowledging and committing to change the bad habits of the past. Typically, it's not enough for a few individuals or teams to adopt this way of thinking, as big changes need cross-functional support to be implemented. For most companies, the ultimate goal is nothing less than an organizational transformation.

Yes, this approach works. And it works because it's grounded in timeless principles that are mostly applied common sense. But it only works with disciplined application. There is no shortcut. Going through the motions is not enough and may actually hide the fact that things haven't really changed.

One of our biggest disappointments is seeing clients where a handful of people adopt this language and framework, but don't really change their way of thinking. They continue avoiding the difficult questions about value and differentiation or continue accepting industry standard segmentations. Needless to say, that approach doesn't work. Only consistent and honest application of the principles and the thinking behind them will make a difference.

While winning, market-back strategic ideas can come from anywhere in the organization, executive leadership plays a critical role in developing, refining, and implementing these strategies. In fact, we believe that leadership commitment is a foundational element of a Grassroots Strategy capability.

This figure shows the relationship between the other key elements of making this a repeatable, differentiating asset for your company:

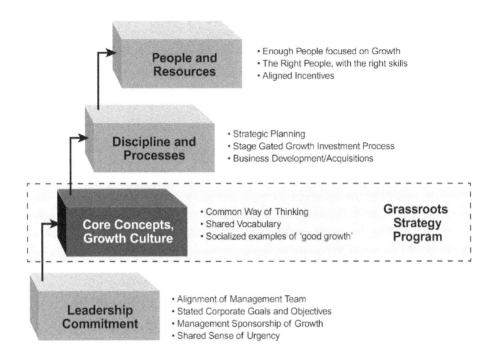

In our experience, all of these elements are required and need to work in concert. Companies looking for a quick fix may focus on only one aspect, but they will rarely achieve the desired results.

Leadership Commitment

Business executives must realize that transforming an organization to strategically grow using market-back principles not only takes time, it requires a different kind of leadership. If you grew up in a hierarchical organization where leaders give orders and the rest follow, you will need to learn some new skills.

The reason is what we call the fundamental paradox of strategic growth:

> *You cannot order people to come up with better strategic growth ideas and do it on your timetable.*
>
> Or the corollary:
>
> *It is disingenuous to expect someone else to come up with the great idea that you can't come up with yourself.*

This difference bears repeating. You can order someone to turn in their expense report by Friday, and maybe even threaten to withhold their reimbursement check if they don't comply. But you cannot order someone to come up with the next great product idea by the end of the week.

Yet, too many companies unwittingly try to force innovation using the management tools and techniques that work in the rest of their business. Invariably, they end up with incremental, low risk ideas and no big wins. Thinking differently and questioning implicit assumptions takes time and in some organizations, courage.

As a leader, your role is not to order innovation to happen. It is to create an environment where good ideas bubble up with as little internal friction as possible. As the name implies, Grassroots Strategy is a bit like gardening: you can provide the right soil, water, and nutrients, but you do not know in advance exactly when the plants will start to sprout or which will end up being the tallest. And like gardening, it requires patience. For the first few days it is impossible to tell if that little green sprout is the tomato plant you want or a weed that you don't.

Measuring Success

For many, this transformation starts by defining what growth means for your organization. In our experience, "good growth" meets several criteria. None of these will surprise you if have read the preceding chapters.

- It is consistent with your strategy and overall capabilities (leverages your differentiation).

- It grows the bottom line, not just the top line. If you have historically measured commercial success primarily based on revenue growth or market share, then this will require some adjustment.

- It is sustainable, or at least not easily copied.

- It is supported by a business model that can turn good growth into profit. This can be either your current business model or one that you intend to build.

In addition to defining good growth, leaders can expand where their organizations look for growth. Teams will often look where they are most comfortable and when they do, they will likely only discover incremental product improvements for existing customers. Sometimes a forcing function is needed to get deeper insights.

We are reminded of the old joke about a police officer slowly making his rounds in the wee hours of the morning. He comes upon a disheveled man in a deserted parking lot, crawling around on his hands and knees in the circle of light created by a lone street lamp. The police officer gets out of his squad car, approaches the man, and asks him what he is doing.

The man, who has obviously been drinking, responds that he is looking for his car keys. When the officer asks if he lost them near this location, the drunk replies, "No, I dropped them back there near the bar, but the light is better here."

Drunkenness aside, your team may need encouragement and support to get out from under their own streetlamp and venture out into the dark. They could talk to non-customers, for example, or study analogous businesses to challenge existing business models. It may be a bit scary and they may not come back with the car keys on the first try, but it's well worth the effort.

Many companies may not realize the inertia they need to overcome to become market oriented. The problem is that most business processes are internally focused. Market-back may make perfect sense to you but for most of your employees, internal deadlines and deliverables define their world: budgets, meetings, performance reviews, etc. Clearly, these things won't go away but in general, they are not the way to define and position your offerings.

It may seem obvious, but you have to put your money where your mouth is. No matter how often you say you support market-back principles, your teams still live with the reality of deadlines and constrained budgets. If you don't actively free up time and budget, change will be paralyzingly slow or non-existent. Worse, these signals tend to say more than your words about what the organization really values.

We have seen countless initiatives grind to a halt because no mid-level manager would stick their neck out and approve travel budgets for VoC ("You want to go talk to customers and intentionally not come back with an order? Are you crazy?"). As a leader, you need to take the risk out of these decisions and make it easier for people to do the right thing.

At many companies we have found that leaders must also teach the basics, leading the entire organization to adopt and live the language of Grassroots Strategy and customer value. In organizations that have rolled out a new fad every couple of quarters, it will take some persistence to overcome the built-up skepticism.

Existing policies and procedures tend to have amazing staying power. If they are not aligned with market-back thinking, it is your job to change them! History suggests that when there is a conflict between existing processes and a new way of thinking, you cannot simply trust that people will figure it out. Nine times out of ten, they will fall back into their comfort zone of old habits, and market-back thinking will die a slow death.

In addition to freeing up resources for growth and expanding where you look for growth, as a leader you also need to admit what you don't know. Specifically, you don't know what the next great growth strategy is or you wouldn't be asking your team to find it, and you certainly don't know how much it is worth or how long it will take to develop it into a profitable business.

Admitting all this is hard for leaders who have learned that confidence is an important attribute. This is demonstrated in the near-religious devotion to "hitting our numbers" at many companies. Even when the assumptions used to develop those numbers turn out to be fundamentally flawed, it is easier to demand super-human effort or make short-sighted trade-offs than to admit that you were wrong.

Case Study: Finding the Next New Business

One of our earliest clients commissioned a cross-functional team of high-potential mid-level managers and charged them with finding "the next $100 million business." The team worked hard and was very thorough. They were also ruthlessly objective in applying their criteria of strategic fit and market size. In the end, they concluded that they had failed: the best they could come up with was two related businesses that they estimated would each produce about $50 million in revenue.

They were so focused on the internal process that it never even occurred to them that the right question to ask was, "Do we want this $50 million business or nothing?" instead of, "Will this business fit our arbitrary revenue target?" Sadly, the team was dispersed, and dejected, they went back to their day jobs. The epilogue is even sadder.

Checking in with this client three years later, we discovered that a competitor had created a business around one of the two opportunities and it had become a profitable $70 million business for them. Even worse, the other opportunity had been pursued by another competitor that later sold it to an entrepreneur who figured out how to turn it into a franchising model to accelerate growth and it was nearing $200 million in revenue.

As this story highlights, leaders may also have to consciously shift to asking the right questions at the right time. They can support good strategic thinking by asking, "What is our differentiation?" or "Which customers will value this new offering?" instead of only focusing on technical ("Will it work?") or financial ("Is it big enough or profitable enough today?") questions.

Especially in technology-driven companies, it is too easy for an organization to shift to the more comfortable and tangible, "Can we do it?" questions without first adequately answering, "Should we do it?" As we have said several times, the logic of the business case is far more important than the precision of the numbers, especially in the early development of a growth idea.

Another of our clients had invested in documenting and implementing a "stage-gate" process for developing a new products, but they were disappointed with the results a year later. You've probably seen this type of regimented approach where projects are approved through multiple defined gates in order to continue progressing towards launch. For this client, the process was being diligently followed, but had only produced a handful of incremental product tweaks; there were no blockbusters anywhere in the pipeline.

We investigated and found that the CEO, who had a finance background, was heavily engaged in the process. Because of his background, the CEO was asking detailed return on investment questions at stage-gate one! And no one was asking about differentiation or customer value, just "Is it different than our current products?" and "What is the target margin?"

So instead of seeking to expand markets or discover new sources of value, the development teams focused on incremental changes that were easiest to forecast to three decimal places in a spreadsheet. Not only were they missing big opportunities, they were rewarding good spreadsheets rather than real strategic thinking. And where they did have product successes, they were systematically underpricing and leaving money on the table because they were using internal benchmarks and not truly understanding customer value.

Leadership Attributes

There are three attributes demonstrated by leaders who succeed at good strategic growth:

- Celebrate both failure and success
- Create a "growth safe zone"
- Practice managerial restraint

To really shift an organization to a growth position, leaders need to get comfortable celebrating failures along with successes. This need not be a public celebration of bad ideas. At a minimum, it should reward people for killing a bad idea early (provided it is a fact-based decision), allowing you to allocate the resources to efforts that are more likely to succeed.

Have you ever experienced a project that seems to plod on like a zombie, never really getting anywhere but never dying? In all likelihood, it's because the budget was allocated and no one wanted to shut the project down for fear that they would lose the funding, or worse that there may not be another role for them at the company. Leaders need to create a "growth safe zone" to signal a break from the previous internal focus, and objectively evaluate projects from a market-back perspective.

Creating this safe zone addresses one of the biggest organizational and motivational challenges for companies seeking to find growth opportunities. How do you get your best people "give their all" when 50% of these projects will likely fail?

While we don't have a complete answer, it should be obvious that punishment of any kind for killing a bad idea, which many companies do implicitly, will cause your best people to avoid these projects at all costs. That's why we think it is so important to not just tolerate, but encourage failure, assuming it is failure for the right reasons. It is also very helpful to have a visible backlog of growth ideas. This makes it clear that even if one project is cancelled, there are still plenty of promising ideas to work on.

The last attribute of good strategic growth leaders is perhaps the hardest: practicing managerial restraint. You have worked your way into a leadership role because of your good judgment and your willingness to take risks, sometimes with limited data. But your role is different when it comes to growth.

If your development teams are asking you to make every call, they are not learning. Worse yet, over time they will learn to only give you the answers they know you prefer. You must have confidence in the people and processes you have put in place and give them time to run. To use the gardening analogy one last time, you can't pull up the plant to see how the roots are growing.

Especially early in a project's development, leaders need to reflect a bias against intervention, even when it is well-intentioned. Your suggestions can too easily be seen as orders by a project team, which could steer them away from where strategic logic is taking them.

Transitioning to a Strategic Growth Culture

It takes a long time to transition to a growth culture that values good strategic marketing. Existing companies must often undo multiple bad habits. And worse, employees who have been around for a while have grown immune to flavor-of-the-month management fads and quick fixes. They are likely to mouth the new words while in their heart-of-hearts believing "this too shall pass."

Patience is a not a quality typically associated with business leaders, but it is essential to cultural transformation. You will need to communicate far more frequently than you think you should have to. And even more importantly, your actions must be aligned with your words. This is especially important as people watch which behaviors get rewarded and who gets promoted. One misstep, such as firing a project team for missing an interim target, can unravel years of progress in building a more constructive growth culture.

For many leaders, adopting these principles initially feels like a leap of faith because their impact is not immediate. In fact, the initial result may be to slow down projects that had proceeded without this thinking. You will need patience and confidence to get you through.

To summarize, if you are a business leader who wants to transition your organization to a market-back, Grassroots Strategy-driven growth engine, you need to:

- Define what good growth looks like using a common vocabulary built on the principles of Grassroots Strategy

- Broaden where your teams are looking for growth ideas

- Encourage cross-functional cooperation and sharing, since no one has a monopoly on good ideas

- Put your money where your mouth is by aligning existing processes with market-back thinking

- Ask the right questions at the right time and stop rewarding false precision

- Tolerate failure but not sloppy thinking or repeating avoidable mistakes

- Practice restraint – stay out of the details as much as possible, and intervene in a predictable, supportive way

- And perhaps hardest of all, be patient

In our experience, these principles need frequent reinforcement, especially early in the transformation process. So as a leader, it is absolutely critical that you repeat the gospel of Grassroots Strategy at every opportunity and back up your words with actions. Find your own words, of course, but take every opportunity to work these messages into your internal communications, both formal and informal.

- Good growth requires good strategy (there is no magic bullet) and this requires disciplined strategic thinking

- The best opportunities are found in "sweet spots" at the intersection of unmet customer needs and unique capabilities

- The search starts with an honest understanding of your differentiation

- Test strategies "market-back" based on an objective view of customer value; invest in market insight and don't just rely on the sales force

- Segment your markets and develop segment-specific value propositions because different customers value different things

Over time you can repeat these messages less often, as a healthy growth culture learns to do these things routinely and consistently. In organizations that have successfully applied these principles, there is always a cadre of true believers who don't just use the principles in conversation, but internalize them and understand their implications and potential impact.

Before this core group is in place, you will need to provide a forcing function to create a team of trusted and well-placed managers who understand these concepts and know how to coach teams in applying them.

But What if I'm Not a Leader?

For readers who don't consider themselves leaders, at least not yet, stop wondering whether this applies to you. It does. Whether you are a CEO or a product manager with no direct reports, you are a leader. Even if you have no positional authority, you can influence and lead by example. As we have said throughout, hierarchal orders may actually be counter-productive to accelerating this type of change.

Regardless of your position in your organization, use what you have learned in this book to change and improve your company. It will take patience and it will take consistency, but it will work. Telling your boss that he is wrong or that his idea is stupid is probably not a good start, but using this thinking in addition to whatever is required by your day-to-day responsibilities will work. Gradually working these principles into how you set priorities and evaluate projects will get you noticed, in a good way.

So, use these principles as a guide. You may need to tweak the language or sequence to fit your organization and there may still be a required set of templates you need to complete, even if you have begun to question their value. At its heart, Grassroots Strategy is a way of thinking and it is a way that works. Be discreet and be polite, but don't shy away from asking your colleagues if they can describe their target segment and whether they have thought about differentiation or customer value.

Even before you bring these ideas to others, you can apply them to specific projects you are already working on to ensure you are asking the right questions and documenting the answers. Importantly, you will want to capture and document these early successes. For example, here is how you would have traditionally set the price, and here is how you priced it after you understood its value to the customer.

Stick with it. It won't be long before others start asking what you're doing and how they can do it too. You won't have to look too far to find support for higher prices, better targeted offerings, and more effective product launches.

In fact, many of our long-term clients have figured out that these are the exact skills that help them stand out among their peers and get promoted. It's no coincidence that several clients saw their careers take off after they figured out how to apply these concepts to their businesses. Of course, it helps that they were already capable managers and willing learners.

Nothing pleases us more than having people we've worked with become Business Unit General Managers or CEOs. It is always rewarding to help smart people succeed, and it is especially gratifying when they invite us help their new teams learn and apply these principles.

These leaders understand that while these principles are presented as strategy and marketing skills, they are also exactly what is needed in general managers. You may succeed as a functional leader by being internally focused but in order to lead and drive a business, you need to understand customers and how they evaluate alternatives. And, if you know how to systematically turn customer input into growth ideas that become profitable businesses, you are really on to something. Demonstrating these skills in any position and at any stage of your career is a proven way to stand out.

Summary

So this is our final charge. As you think about applying these principles, consider the primary benefits they will provide:

- You can accelerate existing projects by getting the best ideas to a better place, faster

- You can apply a set of proven principles across multiple situations, now and in the future

- You can help build an organizational culture where good ideas get better and bad ideas get killed faster through systematic and widespread application of these principles

But on a deeper and more personal level, there is one more benefit. These principles are a better way to think about the world of growth opportunities. They will make the projects and teams you work with more successful, which in turn makes work more fun and more rewarding.

These principles are also a way to differentiate yourself, putting you in a position to lead by example, champion the process, and teach and encourage your colleagues to hold themselves to a higher standard of strategic thinking. There is no greater way to demonstrate your value to an organization than by making those around you better!

Appendix

A Real-World Case Study

Throughout the book we have used case studies, largely from our own experience, to highlight specific portions of the framework. But the magic of Grassroots Strategy is in how the pieces fit together. So, we thought it best to end with a comprehensive example that shows how ideas evolve and improve through the process.

Our typical client engagement includes a five-day Grassroots Strategy session attended by three or four project teams, each with a unique business challenge that needs to be addressed. Each team works with a strategy coach as they learn the principles and concepts of strategic growth and then apply them to their project over the week and beyond.

Every project that goes through a Grassroots Strategy session begins with a charter that describes the current situation and identifies key questions to be answered. The project sponsor chooses a cross-functional team of five to eight people from marketing, sales, engineering, support, operations, etc., to attend the session and drive the project. This chartering process typically starts three to four weeks before the actual multi-day face-to-face session.

Importantly, the project is not over at the end of the session. As we discussed in Chapter 10 (Hypothesis Testing), we develop hypotheses during the week, but it is premature to act on them before testing through market insight. So there is typically a project follow-up period with checkpoints at 30 and 60 days.

Then at roughly 90 days, the project team presents their findings and recommendations to the project sponsor.

The structure of a full Grassroots Strategy program looks like this:

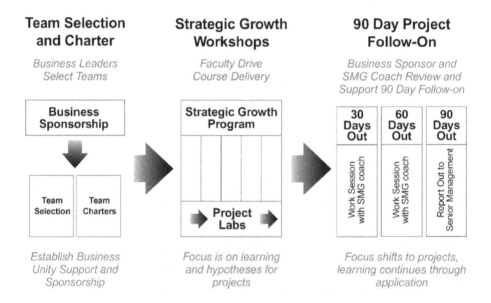

During the face-to-face portion, the teams are taught the Grassroots Strategy framework and concepts through a combination of lecture, stories, and cases. Each learning module is followed by the application of the concepts to the business projects in breakout sessions.

Then each team presents their work to the other teams for feedback. There are optional modules beyond the core Grassroots Strategy framework, but a typical five-day session looks something like this:

Monday	Tuesday	Wednesday	Thursday	Friday
• Introduction	• Project Lab: Report Out	• Project Lab: Report Out	• Project Lab: Report Out	• Overview - winning through The Business Model
• Overview				
• Review Team Charters	• Economic Thinking	• Market Segmentation Challenges and Examples	• Market Insight/ VOC Best Practices	• Project Lab: Report Out
• Marketing Framework	• Lunch		• Lunch	• Presentation To Senior Management
• Introductory Case	• Consumer Value	• Lunch	• VOC Simulation	
• Lunch	• Customer Value mini-case	• Segmentation (continues)	• Value Pricing	• Close - Hard stop at Noon
• Marketing Analysis: Definition, Sizing, and Drivers, Value Mapping	• Project Lab: Customer Value; Value Elements, Value Equation	• Value Proposition	• Project Lab: Planning the next 90 Days	
• Project Lab: revisit Charter/ Market Definition/ Market Drivers/ Value Map		• Integrating Case		
		• Project Lab: Segmentation & Value Proposition		

Background

Let's examine one client's journey through the Grassroots Strategy experience. The specifics of this case are disguised to protect their strategy. We will also share the results and while the numbers are fictional, the relative magnitude and the timing of the impact are completely accurate.

As background, our client sells a filtration media that is used to purify their customers' high-value end products. They had been an early innovator and leader in this market, but lost ground over the years. At the time of their Grassroots Strategy session, they were not profitable and had a very small (less than 1%) share of a market that was over $1 billion in annual sales.

Because of their small market share, they typically competed on price for every possible opportunity. Amazingly, they continued to lose sales most of the time, even though they were often priced at a mere 20% of the market leader. You read that right, they were discounting 80% off the price of the competition (the next best alternative) and still losing most of the time.

But there was a glimmer of hope. Sometimes they won, and those customers who bought from them were both loyal and very happy. The key question was whether they could turn this into a profitable business.

Because the current volume was not covering their fixed costs, they were prepared to shut down the product line if they couldn't find a way to improve the business performance. The lingering question was why some customers were buying from them when the majority of the market had no apparent interest in their offering. Did they have some differentiation and was there a segment of the market that valued what was unique about their product? That was our challenge as we started the week.

Opportunity Definition

The first step in the Grassroots Strategy framework is opportunity definition. After much debate, the team decided that the problem they solve is molecular purification. The value map was relatively simple: they sold material directly to the customer and it was used in a processing step in a larger purification process. The only complication was that they didn't make the processing equipment. They agreed that partnering with an equipment manufacturer was one possible avenue for growth.

Upon drawing their market "cube," they realized another avenue for growth might be shifting away from selling pounds of filtration media to selling an outcome for the customer. In other words, they could potentially get paid based on the amount of the customer's end product that was produced, rather than on the pounds of material used to purify the end product. Periodically replenishing the filtration media could then be sold as a service. If the market was big enough, this could be rolled out as a new business model.

The team also added some details on profit flow to the value map, and confirmed their instinct that the total price of filtration media was a tiny fraction of the cost of a batch of their customers' end product. They had enough financial information to understand that the customer was making very high margins on their end-product (80% or more), so quality and throughput were likely much more important than saving a little money on filtration.

Customer Value

The next day our discussion shifted to customer value. As you recall, customer value is created based on points of differentiation and/or opportunity. The team filled three full flip chart pages with possible value dimensions. As you can imagine, there was a lot of optimism in the room.

Then we categorized each value dimension as described in chapter 5 (Customer Value):

- **(P)** Point of **Parity:** The minimum needed to compete

- **(D)** Point of **Differentiation:** Where they were better than the competition

- **(D-)** Point of **Negative Differentiation:** Where the competition is better than them

- **(O)** Point of **Opportunity:** Things no one is doing, but that would create a lot of value if they could do it

The team then realized that they needed one more category:

- **(P-)** Point of **Negative Parity:** Things the customer expects that they couldn't deliver and thus, the customer would never by from them

At this point, the earlier enthusiasm was quickly waning.

This exercise was a rude awakening. The air seemed to leave the room because as they went through all of their value dimensions, the team found that most of them were P (parity). Of those that weren't P, the majority were D- (negative differentiators). So, for the majority of customers they were no better than the competition on most dimensions, and unfortunately they were worse on some others.

Is it any wonder they were losing sales the majority of the time? Even a deep price discount wasn't enough to overcome the substantial value being created by their competitor. The team was understandably disheartened and ready to call it a day. They were seriously considering recommending shutting down the business.

That's when we reminded them that some customers were consciously choosing to buy from them. Why? Did they have a different set of needs? After some spirited discussion, the team concluded that there was indeed something unique about those customers.

Their current customers' products all had a molecular size and structure that were easily and efficiently filtered with their media. By using competing materials, the customer would need to have two distinct processing steps to get to the required level of purity in their end product. Those processing steps are expensive: around $1 million in additional capital equipment for each step. In addition, each filtration step also introduced about 10% yield loss.

Thus, for certain molecular sizes and structures, our client's material created substantial value relative to the other materials on the market. Not only was their material worth as much as the competing materials, it was worth more than twice the current price of those materials.

No wonder those customers were buying from them! They were no doubt thrilled to pay 20% of what a competitor would have charged for a material that couldn't do the job. The excitement in the room was palpable. What a change from just a couple of hours earlier!

Segmentation

Our discussion focused on segmentation during the third day of the Grassroots Strategy session. As you recall, the first step in segmentation is to identify what you are segmenting. The most obvious thing to segment is customers, but that is not always best. Your segmentation should be done at the level where your differentiation creates value.

Can you tell based on the customer whether they will need your material? In this case no, as some larger customers produce many different sizes and types of molecules as their end products. What determined the places where they were most differentiated and therefore the best fit had nothing to do with the company. It was all about the molecule in the application.

Thus, the segmentation is based on the value, size, and type of molecule. Even if the molecule is the right size and type, if its value is low, then the price our client could charge is correspondingly low because the additional yield is worth proportionally less. The ideal applications involve a high-value molecule that fits the size and type profile where their filtration media would work best.

In our Grassroots Strategy sessions, we like to have a little fun naming segments, which helps to break up a sometimes lengthy and convoluted process. For reasons lost to history, the team named their segments after different types of footwear based on the molecule value and its fit with their filtration media. (This is far from the strangest naming scheme we have seen.)

Here's what they came up with.

Low value molecules where their filtration media wasn't a good fit were named the Flip Flops. High value molecules where their media wasn't a good fit were named the Stilettos.

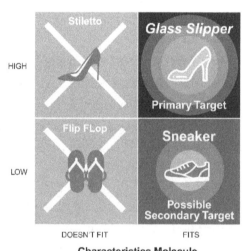

Low value molecules where their media was a good fit were named the Sneakers, and this was identified as a possible secondary target.

The primary target, which was high value molecules where their media was the best fit, was named the Glass Slippers – the proverbial "perfect fit."

Value Proposition

Now that we had both a value equation and a segmentation, they could develop a value proposition for their target segment, the Glass Slipper. Here was their value proposition hypothesis for the Glass Slipper segment.

For *Glass Slipper Applications*
(target customer/segment)

that need *to purify their high-value product with the least possible losses,*
(the problem(s) we solve)

our *OncePure solution*
(the offering that you deliver)

provides *$2M in savings per production line per year*
(quantified value)

unlike *other available purification materials.*
(the next best alternative)

We do this by *providing superior molecule and size selectivity*
(how do we do it)

as demonstrated by *beta tests with key customers.*
(proof points)

At the end of our session on Wednesday, which is typically our longest day, the team was feeling quite good about where things stood. They were starting to believe that they had the makings of a winning strategy, and everyone was both exhilarated and exhausted.

The next two days would define the frameworks for testing the hypothesis, adjusting the price appropriately, and delivering a better performing business. Then the unexpected happened.

On Thursday morning, the VP of Sales, who happened to be on the team, came into the room and proclaimed, "We just received an order and we need to decide what to do." There was no time for market research or lab studies. They needed to decide there and then how they were going to respond.

They set about evaluating the situation by asking these questions:

- How much was the order? *$200,000.*

- Did the molecule fit the target segment? *Yes.*

- How much would the competitor have charged? *Best estimate was $1 million.*

- Would the competitor's material work? *No, it would require taking two processing steps at $1 million each.*

- Would there be a loss of product with the additional processing step? *Yes, most likely 10%.*

- How much was the customer buying of their other offerings? *Not much.*

At this point the question was no longer whether they should raise the price, but rather how much they could raise the price and still be credible. The CEO, COO, and CMO were all consulted, and the decision was made to call the customer and communicate the new, much higher price.

Now this wasn't just any price increase. Here is how the call went:

Client: Thank you for your recent order for our purification media. We would really like to do business with you but as it turns out, we are considering getting out of this business because we are losing money. I hate to be the bearer of bad news, but the only way we can accept this order is for $1.5 million.

Customer: Wait a minute! You quoted me $200,000 for the material.

Client: Yes, I know we did, but we can't accept the order at that price.

Customer: Well, I am very upset, but we really need the material. If we sign a five-year agreement, can we get a 10% discount off that price?

Client: I'll have to get back to you on that.

The next day they received a purchase order for the full $1.5 million. Obviously, this was a risky approach, but it demonstrates the power of really understanding your value and properly segmenting your customers instead of pricing to the average.

Summary

Understanding value gives you the confidence to price correctly, even if customers complain. In this case, it helped that our client had little to lose. What better validation of your value proposition than when a customer agrees to a price increase beyond anyone's wildest imagination and continues to buy?

During the 90-day project follow-up period, the team did additional research to confirm that their hypothesis was basically correct. Over time, they got better at identifying in advance which specific molecular applications were a good fit for their offering.

Over the next three years, this unprofitable business with less than 1% market share raised prices by an average of 500%, grew unit volume by over 300%, became extremely profitable, and achieved greater than 10% market share in their target segment. That is the power of Grassroots Strategy!

Acknowledgements

This book has been thirty years in the making, as every consulting experience has shaped our thinking, refined our ability to communicate these concepts, and contributed to our library of examples. As such, it is impossible to list everyone who has influenced us along the way, but we do need to call out those who loom large.

First and foremost is Dr. Stewart Bither. Stew has been a friend, advisor, dinner partner, and confidante since 2003. He was incredibly patient and magnanimous when we started working together and had far more to learn from him than he could gain from us. He is credited where we have copied directly from his prior work, but there is literally nothing in this book that has not been tested, shaped, or polished by Stew's thoughtful insight and feedback, usually delivered over a few glasses of delicious red wine.

And then there is Rhonda Germany. Rhonda was our client at Honeywell for over 13 years. She gave us the chance to teach this material before we really knew what we were doing. Only because of her patience and support were we able to persevere and produce the body of work we have today. Her countless hours of work behind the scenes delivered the right people and projects to make our sessions there successful, and contributed many of the stories captured herein.

Many other Amphora Consulting clients are also noteworthy for their support and patronage over the years. Several even offered feedback on early manuscripts. Without loyal clients like Mark Sullivan, Pete Smith, Michael Stubblefield, Don Gottwald, Bjorn Hofman, Joanna Sohovich, Tim Martin, and Kees Ver Haar, we would not have been able to keep food on the table while gaining the experience to write this book.

This book would look nothing like its current version without the diligence and commitment of our editor, Donna Guardino, and our fact-checker extraordinaire, David Svigel. Both went above and beyond the call of duty to shape our thinking into something readable.

We also owe a big thank you to all the people who have worked with us over the years as part of Amphora Consulting, starting with our partner, Nick Demos, and our other colleagues, Barrie Berg, Mark Hoffman, Steve Wheeler, Brian Hughes, Frank Bogaert, David Simon, Mike Connors, Gannesh Bharadhwaj, Brad Bodwell, Christine Shea, Soo Hong, Rhett Metz, Jonathan Baker, Chris Thomas, Ron Bruggeman, Hope Bennett, Marty Salva, Paul Kostolansky, Tara Burdick, and Lee Ann Cochran.

Jeff would like to thank the people at the former Booz, Allen and Hamilton who taught him strategy consulting as a craft, particularly Steve Wheeler, Frank Bogaert, Paul Branstad, and Cesare Mainardi.

Darrin deeply appreciates his former partners at FutureSight Consulting, Bruce Scheer and Wes Wernette, who helped him break out of the corporate world and into consulting. Darrin also thanks his father, David Fleming, whose entrepreneurial passion and success inspired him greatly.

Lastly, we both owe a huge debt of gratitude to our families and friends. Without their consistent and loving support, encouragement and sacrifice, this book would never have happened.

Bibliography

Adams, C. (2013, June). *Wheel & Brake Repair and Overhaul.* Retrieved from Aviation Maintenance Magazine: https://www.avm-mag.com/wheel-brake-repair-and-overhaul/

Alden, R., & Tiku, N. (2008, September 1). *How I Did It: Rick Alden, Skullcandy.* Retrieved from www.inc.com: https://www.inc.com/magazine/20080901/how-i-did-it-rick-alden-skullcandy.html

Anderson, J., & Narus, J. (1998). Business Marketing: Understand What Customers Value. *Harvard Business Review.*

Atlas, W. (2019). *The World's Largest Employers.* Retrieved from www.worldatlas.com: https://www.worldatlas.com/articles/the-world-s-largest-employers.html

Beattie, A. (2018, May 15). *What recognized CEO earned the moniker "Neutron Jack"?* Retrieved from www.investopedia.com: https://www.investopedia.com/ask/answers/09/neutron-jack-welch-ceo-general-electric-ge.asp

Best, R. (1997). *Market-Based Management.* Pearsoh.

Bishop, T. (2017, February 9). *The cost of convenience: Amazon's shipping losses top $7B for first time.* Retrieved from www.geekwire.com: https://www.geekwire.com/2017/true-cost-convenience-amazons-annual-shipping-losses-top-7b-first-time/

Blood, B. (2015, December 19). *How does Apple make money?* Retrieved from www.quora.com: https://www.quora.com/How-does-Apple-make-money

Bloomberg. (2019, May 31). *Company Overview of Nest Labs, Inc.* Retrieved from Bloomberg: https://www.bloomberg.com/research/stocks/private/snapshot.asp?privcapId=142508766

Bureau, U. C. (n.d.). *https://factfinder.census.gov.*

Cain, T. (2014, May 28). *Large SUV Sales in America - 2008 Year End.* Retrieved from www.goodcarbadcar.net: http://www.goodcarbadcar.net/2014/05/usa-large-suv-sales-figures-2008-year-end/

Collins, D., & Rukstad, M. (2008). Can You Say What Your Strategy Is? *Harvard Business Review.*

Comstock, O. (2014, January 28). *Most homes have central thermostats on heating and cooling equipment.* Retrieved from U.S. Energy Information Administration: https://www.eia.gov/todayinenergy/detail.php?id=14771

Forbes. (2018, October 3). *The Definitive Ranking Of The Wealthiest Americans.* Retrieved from www.forbes.com: https://www.forbes.com/forbes-400/#2c20bc097e2f

Fortune. (2017). *Global 500.* Retrieved from www.fortune.com: http://fortune.com/global500/

Frieberg, K., & Frieberg, J. (1996). *Nuts!; Southwest Airlines' Crazy Recipe for Business and Personal Success.* Bard Books.

Griswold, A., & Karaian, J. (2018, February 1). *It took Amazon 14 years to make as much in net profit as it did last quarter.* Retrieved from Quartz: https://qz.com/1196256/it-took-amazon-amzn-14-years-to-make-as-much-net-profit-as-it-did-in-the-fourth-quarter-of-2017/

Gross, D. I. (n.d.). *Build Value Understanding.* Retrieved from Institute for the Study of Business Markets (ISBM): https://isbm.smeal.psu.edu/education/value-delivery-framework/build-value-understanding

Haidt, J. (2013). *The Righteous Mind; Why Good People are Divided by Politics and Religion.* Vintage Books.

Kampf, P. (2016). *What are the relative braking contributions from wheel brakes, spoilers and thrust reversers?* Retrieved from Aviation Stock Exchange: https://aviation.stackexchange.com/questions/24579/what-are-the-relative-braking-contributions-from-wheel-brakes-spoilers-and-thru

Kessle, S. (2011, Dec 15). *Nest: The Story Behind the World's Most Beautiful Thermostat.* Retrieved from Mashable: https://mashable.com/2011/12/15/nest-labs-interview/

Kremkau, B. (2007, October 10). *Product Review: Skullcandy Headphones.* Retrieved from ReadJunk:

https://www.readjunk.com/articles/product-review-skullcandy-headphones/

Lanning, M., & Michaels, E. (1988). *A Business is a Value Delivery System.* McKinsey.

Leard, B., & Linn, J. (2016, February). *How Do Gasoline Prices Affect New Vehicle Sales?* Retrieved from Resources : https://www.resourcesmag.org/common-resources/how-do-gasoline-prices-affect-new-vehicle-sales/

Mangalindan, J. (2012, July 30). *Amazon's Recommendation Secret.* Retrieved from www.Fortune.com: http://fortune.com/2012/07/30/amazons-recommendation-secret/

Miller, C. (2017, January 11). *Apple on track to hit $1 trillion in total revenue from iOS by the middle of this year.* Retrieved from www.9to5mac.com: https://9to5mac.com/2017/01/11/apple-1-trillion-in-revenue-from-ios/

Moore, G. (1991). *Crossing the Chasm: Marketing and Selling High-Tech Products to Mainstream Customers .* Harper Business Essentials.

Natanson, E. (2017, September 5). *Amazon Spark - A Social Network for Product Discovery.* Retrieved from www.forbes.com: https://www.forbes.com/sites/eladnatanson/2017/09/05/amazon-spark-a-social-network-for-product-discovery/#47bd0a3191f9

Nordhaus, W. (2007). Two Centuries of Productivity Growth in Computing. *The Journal of Economic History.*

Reiner, R. (Director). (1984). *This Is Spinal Tap* [Motion Picture].

Rumelt, R. (2011). *Good Strategy Band Strategy: The Difference and Why It Matters.*

Schleckser, J. (2018, August 28). *Why Southwest Has Been Profitable 45 Years in a Row.* Retrieved from www.inc.com: https://www.inc.com/jim-schleckser/why-southwest-has-been-profitable-45-years-in-a-row.html

U.S. Energy Information Administration. (2018, May). *RESIDENTIAL ENERGY CONSUMPTION SURVEY (RECS).* Retrieved from U.S. Energy Information Administration: https://www.eia.gov/consumption/residential/data/2015/hc/phphp/hc6.1.php

USAToday. (n.d.). *About USA Today.* Retrieved from www.usatoday.com: http://static.usatoday.com/about/timeline/

USEIA. (n.d.). *Petroleum & Other Liquids Spot Prices.* Retrieved from U.S. Energy Information Administration: https://www.eia.gov/dnav/pet/pet_pri_spt_s1_d.htm

Winkler, R., & Wakabayashi, D. (2014, January 13). *Google to Buy Nest Labs for $3.2 Billion.* Retrieved from The Wall Street Journal: https://www.wsj.com/articles/google-to-buy-nest-labs-for-32-billion-1389648107